# BIRDING

### FOR

# BOOMERS

# BIRDING
## FOR
# BOOMERS

### And Everyone Else Brave Enough to Embrace the World's Most Rewarding and Frustrating Activity

## Sneed B. Collard III

MOUNTAINEERS
BOOKS

# For Lola—Good dog!

**MOUNTAINEERS BOOKS** is dedicated to the exploration, preservation, and enjoyment of outdoor and wilderness areas.

1001 SW Klickitat Way, Suite 201, Seattle, WA 98134
800-553-4453, www.mountaineersbooks.org

Printed in China

First edition, 2024

Design and layout: Jen Grable
Illustrator: Tanner Barkin

Library of Congress Cataloging-in-Publication Data is on file for this title at https://lccn.loc.gov/2024004607. An ebook record is available at https://lccn.loc.gov/2024004608.

Please use common sense. It is incumbent upon any user of this guide to assess their own skills, experience, and fitness; to assume responsibility for their own actions and safety; to recognize the inherent dangers in outdoor and wilderness environments and travel; and to be responsible stewards of birds and bird habitats. The publisher and author are expressly not responsible for any adverse consequences resulting directly or indirectly from information contained in this book.

Printed on FSC-certified materials

ISBN (paperback): 978-1-68051-670-8
ISBN (ebook): 978-1-68051-671-5

*An independent nonprofit publisher since 1960*

# CONTENTS

# PART VII

## GIVING BACK TO BIRDS

## A Note on Quotations

While the author certifies that the quotations within chapters of the main text are, to the best of his knowledge, reliable, he can almost guarantee that quotes attributed to famous people at the beginning of each section have been altered and should be viewed with deep suspicion. Thank you.

## How to Use This Book

In this guide, I have presented topics in the order that a beginning birder would naturally encounter or want to learn about them. However, this book is not a *novel*. Feel free to jump around from topic to topic to your heart's content—but before you need a triple-bypass surgery.

# PART I

# BIRDING: A BOOMER PERSPECTIVE

*We choose to go birding in this decade and do the other things not because they are easy, but because they are hard, because birding will serve to organize and measure the best of our energies and skills.*
*—John F. Kennedy*

**CHAPTER 1**

# Glorious, Infuriating Spring

I begin each spring birding season full of youthful hope and optimism. The buds start to plump out on my deciduous shrubs and trees in preparation for a full-scale burst of leaf and flower. As temperatures warm and daylight lengthens, I swap out my down jacket for a sweatshirt and nylon shell. Chickadees begin singing and investigating the birdhouse in the front yard. Northern Flickers and Pileated Woodpeckers start drumming. And then, glory of all glories, the first migrant songbirds show up.

In our neighborhood in Montana, American Robins make the first big splash. Robins may not seem like a big deal, but the more I've observed and learned about these handsome birds, the more I've come to appreciate what hardy survivors they are. Not only have they adapted to human civilization with skill, they tolerate freak storms and temperature extremes with aplomb. But for me, the best thing about robins is that I can recognize their songs!

Throughout the long winter, I practice picking out the varied sounds of our resident species: chickadees, nuthatches, finches and House Sparrows, Black-billed Magpies, and of course my namesake, Eurasian Collared-Doves. When robins arrive, well, it's just great. I add their songs to my mental library and enjoy how their vocalizations fill out the chorus.

Alas, for a Boomer like me, their song also foretells a season of doom and despondency.

As each subsequent species arrives, it adds to the audio mix. Unfortunately, even with my hearing aids cranked up, these newcomers often don't have the distinct "cheery-up, cheery, cheery-up" kind of melody I can recognize. Instead, they belt out *tseeps* and rattles and triplets, many of them at—or beyond—the limits of both my hearing abilities and my mental capacities to distinguish them.

At first, I hang in there, I pick out the *chubby chubby chubby* of the Ruby-crowned Kinglet and the three- or four-part composition of the Song Sparrow. I am able to relearn the repeating sweetness of Yellow-rumped Warblers and savor the grassland call of the meadowlark. With the arrival of each new wave, however, it becomes harder for me to tell songs apart, and by early May I have begun a spiraling descent into confusion, frustration, and dismay.

Forest birding is the worst. When my son, Braden, and I go into the woods, he starts exclaiming, "Did you hear that? Townsend's Warbler!" Or "You know that one, don't you? Black-headed Grosbeak!" I try to keep

up. Really, I do. But the Townsend's sounds like what I thought a Yellow-rumped sounds like, and I mistake the grosbeak for a Western Tanager or Cassin's Vireo.

It all ends badly. Very badly. After an hour I either snap at my son for having such a great brain and perfect sensory systems, or I slump to the ground, gorging on chocolate and weeping so copiously that the salt from my tears kills the five-hundred-year-old ponderosa pine next to me, incurring a fine from the US Forest Service for destroying a national treasure.

If this situation seems familiar to you, I can offer only one comforting sentiment: it's not your fault.

Though it is with great pleasure that I see more and more young people getting into birding, if you are reading this you can probably recall that this wasn't the case when we were kids. You may not have heard anyone even mention birding—unless it was to make some snarky comment about "those kooky bird-watchers" or laugh while cartoon birders got run over by heavy equipment on Saturday morning television. For those of us who *did* contemplate learning about birds, well, it was something we were going to do when we got older. Maybe even when we retired.

What a bonehead idea—and you know why.

If we wait until later in life to finally take time to enjoy and observe the miraculous wealth of bird life around us, we often confront a major, unsolvable obstacle: we no longer have the faculties to do it. At least not with any kind of ease or grace. For many, our ears are blown from decades of traffic noise, shotgun blasts, and Led Zeppelin. For others, our eyesight has betrayed us, so that what looks like an American Robin to a teenager resembles a loaf of moldy bread sitting on a branch. Even if your senses *have* held up, chances are that your knees, hips, and back have not. A hike up a small hill feels like an assault on Iwo Jima. One that will likely lead to a year's worth of chiropractor visits, or worse, replacement of every joint in your sorry skeleton. A walk through the snow, and your body may not recover until spring.

And folks, we haven't even *mentioned* our brains yet.

As much as I'd like to deny it, my brain just doesn't compute like it did forty years ago. I studied marine biology in college, and looking back, I am astounded I was able to absorb all the scientific names that I learned as an undergraduate. I can't say it was as easy for me as it was for others, but with a little study I managed.

And now? Well, when faced with having to learn a new bird name, I seriously have to contemplate whether it would be a better use of my time to drink a beer. My brain just doesn't want to do it—learn the name, I mean, not drink the beer. It's not simply names, either, which we can admit are a bit abstract. My brain's diminished capacity also impacts my abilities to learn birds' identifying marks or distinguish one bird call from another.

Again, does this sound familiar? If so, welcome to life's "second half," a stage when no matter how many cortisone injections we receive, the ravages of time cannot be denied. So here is my recommendation to those of you who would like to begin birding: don't.

For a middle-aged or older person, birding is simply a hopeless, depressing ambition, one that would be better replaced by watching television, getting divorced, or pursuing your dreams of becoming an alcoholic. In fact, you may as well close this book now and forget about the whole business. . . .

*Just kidding!*

## CHAPTER 2

# A Personal Birdestimony

Even if you can barely hear your alarm clock or limp down the stairs to the kitchen, birding can offer immense joy and satisfaction—perhaps the most you will experience in your later decades. I know because it has done this for me, even though I waited until my mid-fifties to seriously pick up a pair of binoculars.

For most of my life I, like many of you, clung to the mantra "birding is something I'll do later." I would have waited even longer, except that I was blessed with a son who embraced serious avian interests when only ten years old. At first Braden and I simply tried to figure out what was flitting around the yard, but we quickly began going out on hikes and visiting wildlife refuges to see what we might discover. We were greatly inspired by the hilarious movie *The Big Year*, starring three of our favorite actors, Steve Martin, Owen Wilson, and Jack Black, and we decided to embark on our own Big Year adventure, seeing how many species we could rack up in the US and Canada in a single calendar year.

It was one of the best decisions we ever made. Not only did we have countless adventures and make lifelong memories, we accumulated a college degree's worth of birding skills and knowledge in a single twelve-month span.

Unfortunately, the following year, disaster struck. Up until then, my sensory systems had functioned fairly well. Sure, I had suffered moderate tinnitus, or ringing of the ears, since my early twenties, but that didn't seem to impact my ability to hear birdsong. However, the summer after our Big Year, Braden, his birding buddy Nick, and I were all visiting Bowdoin National Wildlife Refuge in eastern Montana. I had pulled over our intrepid minivan so that we could listen at one of the marshy locations around the lake when Nick shouted, "Sedge Wren!"

"I hear it!" Braden joined in.

I had my window rolled down on the correct side of the car and didn't hear a thing. At first I thought I'd just missed it. I *was* the driver, after all, and had other duties to attend to. But when the wren sang again and again, my ears didn't register the tiniest blip.

Over the next few months, I realized that I was missing more and more bird calls, especially in the high frequencies. I tried to tell myself that maybe I had too much earwax buildup, but after getting my ears cleaned, a growing, sinking realization settled in my gut.

My ears were shot.

Looking back, there *had* been warning signs, from my wife's "mumbling" to the fact that my stereo didn't sound as sharp and crisp as I remembered. It wasn't until I had trouble hearing the entire call of a chickadee, however, that the full impact of my loss slammed into me.

I took it badly. I shook my fists at the hearing gods. I cursed my late father for taking me out to shoot shotguns without ear protection. I lamented long evenings listening to the live version of the Rolling Stones' "Midnight Rambler" through headphones with the volume cranked up.

Finally, I got fitted with a pair of hearing aids.

The hearing aids didn't totally solve my problems, but they restored at least some of my abilities. More importantly, they helped me begin to come to terms with my new impairment and figure out how I could continue to enjoy this wonderful activity, even if I could no longer become the Best Birder in the History of the Universe.

This book is my attempt to share what I have learned with all of you who are in a similar boat—if not with your ears, then with your eyes, your brain, your knees, your hips, even your finances. Regardless of whether you are a Boomer like me or a spry twenty- or forty-year-old, whatever *thing* you might be dealing with, I'm here both to offer support, and to provide perspective, strategies, and information to help you shrug off your own inadequacies and boldly pursue one of the world's all-time greatest passions. And what if you are leading a perfect life with perfect health? Well, I hate you already, but this book will provide you with all the essentials you will need to begin, and even excel, at birding too.

Either way, we should first answer a simple question: why bother?

## CHAPTER 3

# Birds: The Key to All Happiness

Okay, this chapter title is just messing with you. As we all know, *food* and *sex* are the keys to all happiness, but if the decades have started piling up on you, it's possible you can no longer indulge in either of those to your satisfaction, so that leaves our next best option: birds. And really, birds are a pretty darned good option to have.

To realize the immense satisfaction of birding, however, you'll have to put down your smartphone—at least for now. I will instruct you to pick it back up later, but for a greater purpose than playing word games or checking stock prices. Right now, simply step to your window and look outside. Do you see any birds? Probably. And that's one of the first great things about birds. They are *everywhere*.

I have never been in an environment that didn't support birds. Granted, in a city, the majority of those birds may be invasive species such as Rock Pigeons, House Sparrows, and European Starlings. But the fact that they can survive in our concrete jungles is remarkable in itself.

Of course, there's more to birding than standing by the window. Once you get outside, and especially when you begin carrying a pair of binoculars, you will notice different kinds of birds in almost every place that you visit, whether it is the local schoolyard, a city park, or the patio of your favorite barbecue joint. You'll say to yourself, "Huh, I wonder what

that bird is," and study its details so you can distinguish it from the bird sitting next to it.

So already, these little winged creatures have stimulated your brain by firing up your powers of awareness and observation. But this is merely prelude. As you pay more attention to birds and inevitably become more interested in them, they will glide into and enrich every aspect of your life, just as they did for me. You'll buy a bird field guide and race home to flip through it after seeing a weird bird perched atop the grocery store. Naturally, you'll forget to put the ice cream in the freezer, so you'll have to return to the store for a fresh carton and a closer look at the weird bird.

Next, you'll invite a friend for a round of golf, hoping that you'll be able to score under ten on the par-four ninth that perpetually bedevils you. After you've torn up twenty yards of turf with your six iron, however, you'll suddenly stop, slack-jawed, as a large pterodactyl-like creature flies overhead, making you forget how much you suck at golf and, ironically, distracting you enough to land your very next shot on the center of the green.

Do you go on vacation? Be honest—do you *enjoy* it? I don't. Not really. I used to, but if you're like me, even the word "vacation" brings up a vague sense of dread and disappointment. Sure, I can still go to new places, visit museums, eat food, look at buildings, but then what? I mean, yeah, it's great that this is where Michelangelo stubbed his toe or James Joyce got the inspiration for *An Excruciatingly Dull Portrait of a Totally Narcissistic Artist as a Young Man*, but really, the main thing I share with Michelangelo and Joyce is that I will soon be joining them in the grave.

Birds, I have discovered, turn travel back into an *adventure*. When the rest of your tour group marches off looking for a six-sided stone in an alley of Cuzco, you can give them the slip and try to discover a Giant Humming-bird or Peruvian Sierra Finch in a nearby park. Instead of whiling away a long layover in the Amsterdam airport stuffing yourself on *poffertjes*, you can hop a train downtown and rack up twenty new species for your life list—the list of all of the bird species you have seen in your lifetime—including Common Wood-Pigeon, Eurasian Blue Tit, and Great Spotted Woodpecker!

Birding can lead to other wonderful things as well. Do you enjoy gardening? Once you start to identify birds and learn where to find them, it may occur to you, "Gee, I wonder if I could put some plants in the yard that birds might like." Don't be surprised to find yourself tearing out those useless ornamental shrubs and trees some feckless landscaper sold you decades ago, and replacing them with native flowering plants that offer food and shelter to your favorite local birds.

A greater interest in birds may even help you develop a greater purpose in life, like protecting certain species for future

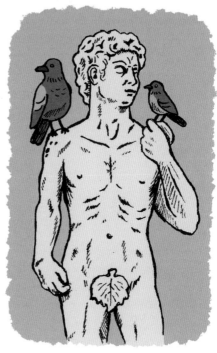

generations. You'll join the National Audubon Society, perhaps, and also discover the great people at the American Birding Association (ABA), the American Bird Conservancy, the Cornell Lab of Ornithology, and other groups making a real difference in protecting our planet.

All of these things—and much, much more—have happened to me, and in just the short decade or so since I began birding.

But I am getting ahead of myself. Let's get back to basics and take a look at how to get started birding, one "second halfer" to another.

# PART II

# THE COURAGE TO BIRD: GETTING STARTED

*We shall bird our island, whatever the cost may be, we shall bird on the beaches, we shall bird on the landing grounds, we shall bird in the fields and in the streets, we shall bird in the hills; we shall never lay down our binoculars, field guides, and spotting scopes.*
*—Winston Churchill*

## CHAPTER 4

# Binoculars: The Key to Great Birding

I had planned to launch this section with a basic tutorial on bird identification, but realized that such a discussion would be pointless if you don't have a couple of essential tools at your disposal. Fortunately, one of the huge advantages of birding compared to, say, driving in NASCAR or building your own intergalactic spaceship, is that birding requires very little money to get started.

Whether you are still working a job or jobs, own a 401K disgorging obscene amounts of cash, or are just eking by on Social Security, birding's financial threshold lies within your grasp. At its most basic, your new activity requires only a decent pair of binoculars and a field guide. Sure, you can and probably will spend more, and later I'll share many recommendations for additional items and expenses, but it's the binocs and book that enable you to leap into your newfound addiction. We'll cover the book in the next chapter; here it's all about the binoculars.

## Binocular Basics

You *can* look at birds without using binoculars—but you won't get very far. Even if you have the best eyes on the planet, most birds are simply too small to examine in detail without some means of magnification. When you begin, you can probably get away with borrowing Cousin Bob's binoculars that he got for free with his subscription to *Hog Hunters* magazine. It's the kind of binoculars I used for many years before I really started taking birding seriously. Eventually, though, you're going to want to either borrow a better pair, or find a way to invest in an upgrade.

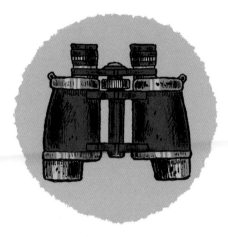

So what do you look for?

Birding binoculars have to meet two requirements: creating a clear, well-lit image and offering enough magnification to see your avian quarry. Most birders I know choose 8 X 42 or 10 X 42 binoculars. The first number, 8 or 10, refers to the magnification, while the second number refers to the diameter in millimeters of the objective lens at the front, or "big end," of the binoculars. Some birders, especially if they have trouble finding objects through their binoculars, prefer a lower magnification of 8 because it gives them a wider field of view, improving the odds of locating a bird. Personally, I appreciate the higher magnification, so I go with 10. I don't recommend going over that, as you'll spend all of your time trying to *find* birds—and they will have fled by the time you pinpoint their locations.

The second number, the diameter of the objective lens, determines how much light the binoculars let in, which, in turn, influences the clarity and quality of the image you see. You can find binoculars with huge objective lenses, but bigger size adds extra weight, and most birders find that 42 is the "sweet spot."

Here are a few other things to consider when making your purchase:

- **Sharpness:** Cheap binoculars have cheap optics that produce fuzzy, poor images, but part of the joy of birding is to see birds in all their glory. I highly recommend trying several brands in an outdoor setting so that you can compare them to Cousin Bob's cheap-o binoculars. This will help you appreciate a truly great, sharp image when you see it.

- **Field of View:** As indicated above, the higher the magnification you have, the narrower your field of view, or how wide an area you can see through your binoculars. Because of this, field of view is fairly standardized, but if you really want binoculars with both high magnification and wide field of view, some companies make them. Just be prepared to pay more.
- **Weight:** Mine weigh about twenty-one ounces, or just over a pound, and I find that more than manageable. Two pounds starts feeling a little heavy after you've lugged them around for two or three hours and hoisted them to your eyes for the six-hundredth time.
- **Waterproofing:** Your binoculars *will* get wet, so if you don't want your view to quickly resemble a petri dish full of water vapor and yet-to-be-discovered pathogenic microorganisms, make sure the binocs come sealed.
- **Warranty:** Some manufacturers offer incredible lifetime, no-questions-asked warranties that can be especially useful. Be sure to ask.

## Getting What You Pay For

Beyond the binoculars' technical specifications, price is an obvious consideration. Again, you *can* find super-cheap binoculars, but in my experience, binocs originally priced below the $200–$300 range probably aren't going to be worth your investment. My son and I both use Nikon Monarch M5 binoculars and have been very happy with them, but Vortex, Bushnell, Vanguard, Celestron, and other companies offer solid products in this price range.

If you can afford to be patient, watch for sales at your favorite retailers, or check your local sporting goods stores, especially at the end of hunting season, to see if they are dumping inventory or getting rid of floor models. I got my first pair of Nikons that way and saved about a third off the price.

One final thought when choosing binoculars is to ask yourself, "How do these feel in my hands?" If, when you pick up the binoculars, a memory of your sweetest lover immediately comes to mind, then baby, those binoculars are for you!

**CHAPTER 5**

# The Birding Field Guide

The second essential tool in any birder's arsenal is the birding field guide. Field guides come in an enormous variety of styles and formats, but each one is basically a catalog of a set of birds. Some specialize in a single type of bird, like birds of prey or warblers. Most field guides, however, focus on all the birds that can be found in a particular area, such as North America, East Asia, California—or even specific places such as Houston, Texas. You will typically find an illustration of each bird, a written description of the bird and how to identify it, notes about its habitat, and a map of where it can be found at various times of the year. Some guides omit one or more of the above or add additional material. But you get the idea.

The original purpose of a field guide was to give birders a handy reference to take with them on any kind of outing. Nowadays, many people prefer not to tote a physical book with them when out walking or hiking and instead rely on a smartphone app (more on that later). That, however, doesn't make a physical field guide any less useful. Even though I usually leave my bound field guides at home or in my car when I'm birding, I refer to them almost daily to help me learn and understand what I am seeing outside.

For most birders, in fact, field guides are an integral part of the birding experience. Why? Because a deep part of the human psyche finds it almost impossible to connect with something without being able to attach a name to it and distinguish it from other things. Birds offer the ultimate proof of concept. Consider the dozens of species of North American sparrows, many of which look identical to a beginning birder. Sparrows without a doubt are what inspired frustrated birders to resort to the catch-all label LBB— Little Brown Bird—for any small nondescript

bird they observed but couldn't identify. But various sparrow species *are* different—often much more than you'd think (see Chapter 21: Tackling Difficult Birds, Group by Group). A field guide provides an entry point to distinguishing, comparing, learning, and enjoying these differences.

Having a bird guide, though, has another important function: preparation.

When we first started birding, Braden spent hours reading his bird guide before bedtime, and at first I thought, "Aw, that's cute how he just really loves birds." When we went out in the field, however, I realized that the book wasn't just helping him distinguish birds we had seen; it was preparing him for the birds we were *going* to see. Within months, when we encountered a new species, he could correctly identify it—or at least point us in the right direction—long before I could, and that was due to his avid bedtime study of the field guide.

Which raises the essential question: *Which guide should you choose?*

## The Birding Bible

The truth is that the longer you bird, the more bird books you will likely acquire—including, I hope, multiple copies of every bird book I have ever written! There are a host of great field guides to identifying birds, including those published by Audubon, National Geographic, Kenn Kaufman,

# Bird Names: Stop the Presses!

As we were going through the final editing process for this book, the American Ornithological Society (AOS) handed down a landmark decision that will send both birders and book publishers scrambling. In the birding world, the AOS assumes responsibility for both scientific and English (or common) names of birds in the Americas. What this means is that the AOS not only gets involved in naming new birds, it is tasked with revising names based on scientific evidence, societal trends—and in some cases, I suspect, serious backroom lobbying efforts. Even in the relatively short time since Braden and I began birding, we've had to learn several new bird names based on AOS decisions: Gray Jay was renamed Canada Jay; McCown's Longspur was renamed Thick-billed Longspur; and, most recently, Mew Gull was renamed Short-billed Gull.

Sometimes, the intent of such changes is to install a name that better reflects the actual characteristics of a bird in the field—though the change of Gray Jay to Canada Jay seriously undermines this argument. In the case of Thick-billed Longspur, the change from McCown's Longspur resulted from the fact that McCown was a Confederate general, and many objected to having a visible symbol of slavery honored in a bird's name. The change of Mew Gull stemmed from the bird being split into two different species: a largely Eurasian bird became Common Gull, while our North American version was renamed Short-billed Gull.

Especially after the change of McCown's Longspur, however, voices in the birding community and the world at large pointed out that many common bird names were problematic—especially some of those named after people. After debating the option of considering these names on a case by case basis, the AOS made a bold decision, issuing the following statement:

*The AOS commits to changing all English-language names of birds within its geographic jurisdiction that are named directly after people (eponyms), along with other names deemed offensive and exclusionary, focusing first on those species that occur primarily within the US or Canada.*

According to an NPR report, this decision will initially affect an astonishing seventy or eighty species, but it could spread further. For personal and historical reasons, I will be sad to see some of these names get tossed into the dumpster—especially Lincoln's Sparrow, Clark's Nutcracker, and Lewis's Woodpecker. I understand the decision, however, and feel like it's probably a good move to simply sweep away these honorifics once and for all.

I do hope, however, that the new names actually reflect useful ID features of the birds—and that the committee gets busy improving a few additional bird names as well. One name that drives me and plenty of other birders crazy, for instance, is "Ringed-neck Duck." Really, you have to be under some serious chemical influences to detect a ring around the neck of this handsome creature. Its bill, on the other hand, has a beautiful white ring around it, so why not change the name to Ring-billed Duck?

Entire books are probably being written about this latest naming development, so I'll stop now. Suffice it to say that many of us will have to learn a whole slew of new bird names in the coming years, and we will probably also have to invest in new North American—and possibly South American—field guides. Field guide publishers won't be complaining about that!

the ABA, Roger Tory Peterson, and others. They cater to every region, age level, and interest, and I own twenty-nine of them at last count. I kid you not! Different guides appeal to different people. Some prefer photos over illustrations. Others value top-quality range maps, while others might prioritize the natural history information about each bird. For Braden and me, however, there is only one "Birding Bible"—the second edition of *The Sibley Guide to Birds* written and illustrated by David Allen Sibley.

One curious thing about a field guide illustrated with drawings or paintings is that the illustrations are often more useful than an actual photograph for identifying a bird. No one has explained this to me, but it must have something to do with how illustrations either emphasize the most important ID features of a bird or zero in on a species' common denominators, cutting through the often frustrating individual variations we birders observe in the wild. Whatever the reason, *Sibley* is the gold standard for bird ID and may be the best investment you ever make.

Like other field guides, *Sibley* also offers range maps, habitat notes, and written descriptions of the birds and their vocalizations—though in my opinion, a written description of a bird's vocalization is as useful as telling someone what a delicious steaming plate of chicken mole tastes like. My one complaint about *Sibley*? The book's cheap spine, which may begin to fall off the moment you breathe on it. In other words, you might want to equip it with your own book cover—but don't let that stop you from buying a copy. Note that David Sibley also has produced versions of his guide specifically for eastern and western North America, but I'd start with the all-encompassing "one-stop" version. It will help you better understand the big picture of North American birds and what they are about, and will be more useful if you are fortunate enough to be able to bird outside your own "home range."

As I implied earlier, *Sibley* and several other field guides also come as handy phone apps, so you don't have to lug the admittedly weighty tome

# Field Guides Abroad

If you are lucky enough to travel outside of North America, I highly recommend picking up a field guide for the area you plan to visit several months before your trip. Studying a guide ahead of time will help familiarize you with what you might see and vastly increase your enjoyment of whatever birding you get to do on your travels. Instead of seeing a bird and thinking, "Oh, that's some kind of songbird," for instance, your brain might register that the bird is some kind of thrush—and even with that bit of information, there's a much better chance you'll be able to arrive at a solid ID.

The one problem with getting field guides for other countries is that you may not have many to choose from. Often, I've found that there really is only one English-language guide of any value for a particular country or region. If a web search doesn't uncover an obvious choice, take a look at the Princeton University Press catalog as it has a wide-ranging selection. Buteo Books also offers a huge variety of field guides and other bird-related books.

around with you when you're out birding. I'll talk more about different kinds of apps in later chapters. Again, though, I heartily recommend that you have at least one or two actual physical bird field guides at your fingertips. A physical book makes it easier to flip back and forth and compare species, and if you don't mind desecrating it, you also can note your sightings in the margins. Besides, aren't you sick to death of staring at screens? I find it a wonderful relief to study an actual book, and my guess is that you, my fellow birders, will too.

## CHAPTER 6

# Braving Bird Identification

Now that you have your essential tools in hand, it's time to actually start birding. How? Well, if you could distill birding down to one fundamental concept, it would be identification. Unless you want to look up at the sky and, like some daisy-addled actress from the 1950s, repeat "Oh, look at the pretty birds" over and over, your primary task—at least for the first year or two of your birding career—will be to distinguish Bird A from Bird B. And Bird C from D. And, well, with almost eleven thousand bird species currently recognized on Earth, not even the Chinese language character set will cover this line of thought.

Bird identification almost universally seems like a daunting task for a beginning birder, but do not be cowed! The good news is that you do not need to learn to identify all eleven thousand species of birds at once, or even at all. After almost a decade of birding, for instance, I have concluded that I will be pretty well satisfied if I can distinguish, say, 10 percent of that number when I draw my final breath.

The news gets better. Your neighborhood, where you will spend most of your birding hours, is unlikely to have more than a couple hundred species throughout *an entire year*, and usually far fewer than that. So in a flash, your first goal is to learn a mere two or three dozen kinds of birds, a manageable task for even a crusty Boomer like me.

Many field guides provide primers on bird identification, while many more books, apps, blogs, and other online resources go into as much detail and specificity as you could ever want. It is *way* beyond the scope of this book to cover this wealth of resources. However, since you currently are reading *this* book—and not those other resources—it's worth spending a few pages on how to grapple with the intimidating task of bird ID right now.

Several bird features allow you to zoom in on the species you're looking at, or at least narrow it down to a handful of possibilities. Generally, they are size, shape, coloration, habits, habitat, vocalizations, time of year, and geographic location—in other words many of the same features you use to identify your friends, spouse, children, and grandchildren. To ease into bird identification, let me present a real-world example of how it typically unfolds . . .

## Your First ID

Let's say you're walking your dog in a nearby park and you see a medium-sized bird sifting through fallen leaves. Its middling size and kind of roundish, chubby shape remind you of a robin—which is an important lesson in itself. After all, most of us recognize a few kinds of birds, whether or not we've been paying attention, and those birds can serve as important reference points.

Anyway, you're thinking, "Hm . . . I know a robin has a red breast and this bird doesn't, so it's probably not a robin." That's when you also notice the bird is kind of brown overall and has dark spots on a pale breast. Perhaps that will be enough to identify it?

After excitedly dragging Fido home against his will, you race to open up your bird field guide. You're not sure where to look, so you turn to American Robin and confirm that it was *not* the bird you saw. Flipping to some adjacent pages, however, your heart beats faster. Why? Because under the category of "thrushes" you come across a bunch of robin-like birds that *could* be your bird. Unfortunately, quite a few of them look the same: Wood Thrush, Veery, Hermit Thrush, Gray-cheeked Thrush, Bicknell's Thrush, and Swainson's Thrush. You despair at so many choices but then notice that the Veery is reddish overall—so you can cross that one off your list.

Same with the Wood Thrush—plus, a Wood Thrush has *really* black spots, and your bird's spots were softer.

Alas, that still leaves you with at least four possibilities.

And then you notice the species range maps.

According to the little color-coded maps under each bird, Bicknell's Thrush lives on the extreme East Coast and you live in Arkansas, so out it goes. "Wait," you think, "what can the range maps tell me for the other species?" You scan through them and make a startling discovery: while Swainson's, Gray-cheeked, and Hermit Thrush all live in Arkansas, the first two pass through *only during migration*, and guess what? It's February—definitely *not* migration season. That means your bird could only be one species—Hermit Thrush. Even better, you confirm this the next time you see the thrush in the park by noting that your bird has a reddish tail and sharper white eye-ring than either Swainson's or Gray-cheeked Thrush.

Congratulations, you have just taught yourself a bird! And believe it or not, this is how bird identification goes, even for birders with years of experience. Nonetheless, let's take a closer look at some of the key features I've just mentioned.

## An ID Poll

Just for fun, I recently created a poll on the Facebook birding page Redpolling (named after a member of the finch family, it's a group specifically dedicated to creating and responding to fun bird-related polls and questions). I asked birders there to choose the first feature that they key in on when out in the field. More than 130 people responded, and here are the results:

- Body shape............................................................56 percent
- Movement (flight and nonflight) ......................16 percent
- Size .....................................................................12 percent
- Color.....................................................................4 percent
- Habitat .................................................................3 percent
- Bill shape..............................................................3 percent
- Behavior (other than movement).........................2 percent

Honestly, these results surprised me. I mean, a bird's color made a first impression on only *4 percent of birders*? How could that be? Perhaps it's because the respondents were mostly experienced birders, and their answers, as one respondent pointed out, would be different than for a beginning birder—a sentiment with which I completely concur. So with that in mind, let's leap into ID features in an order that will be especially relevant to anyone who is just starting out.

## Size

A bird's size tends to be the first thing that registers for most beginning birders—and gives people a first stab at a species ID. When I'm out strolling and see a bird, my brain immediately asks, "Big, medium, or small?" What these categories mean depends on the birder, but being able to throw a bird into a size category can be immensely useful.

If I glance up to see a bird flying overhead, for instance, and my brain shouts "big" then I know I am probably looking at some kind of raptor (hawk, eagle, vulture), wading bird (heron, egret, crane), seabird (cormorant, pelican, gull), or waterfowl (duck, goose, swan). Similarly, if my brain says "small," then I'm going to start considering if it's a finch, sparrow, warbler, chickadee, nuthatch, or another kind of petite songbird. Oh yeah, or hummingbird, but they kind of buzz around in their own category.

Small, as you'll discover, is smaller than most people might think. Many songbirds weigh less than an ounce and would fit neatly into the cup of your hand. An odd feature of small birds is that they often look bigger than they

actually are, so keep that in mind when you're out in the field.

Which brings us to medium—birds that, let's say, are about the size of a can of pop. What makes this category tricky is that almost *all* bird groups have at least a couple of medium-sized representatives. We usually think of raptors (birds of prey) as large, for instance, but American Kestrels, Sharp-shinned Hawks, and a ton of owls are distinctly medium. At the other end of the scale in the overall smaller sparrow group, Fox Sparrows and California Towhees scoot *up* into the medium column. In general, however, calling something "medium" can narrow things down to thrushes, woodpeckers, orioles, blackbirds, grosbeaks, pigeons, doves, grackles, jays, meadowlarks, and a few other groups—a useful first cut in the ID process.

## Color

Again, I was surprised by how low a bird's color ranked in my Redpolling poll results because for many bird groups, colors tell all. The first warblers, tanagers, grosbeaks, orioles, buntings, goldfinches, blackbirds, and thrushes that almost every beginning birder learns are the bright, breeding males that sport stunning, distinct color patterns. Bright colors also are key when identifying many wading birds (herons, egrets, ibises), corvids (jays, magpies, crows, ravens), and male ducks in breeding plumage.

Furthermore, the first, or dominant, color you see—usually on a bird's head, folded wings, or breast—gives you an immediate clue to what you're looking at. You'll quickly learn, for instance, that if you spot a small, bright-yellow bird in your backyard, you are most likely seeing a warbler, tanager, or goldfinch. If the bird flashes blue, you're probably thinking jay, bluebird, bunting, or Blue Grosbeak. If you live in the East, a full-on red body is a dead giveaway for Northern Cardinal, and Summer and Scarlet Tanagers—or if you're in the Southwest, Vermilion Flycatcher.

IDing birds by color does have limitations. For one, females are almost *always* drabber than males—often radically so—so you'll eventually have to learn them too. Colors also change by season. If you learn to recognize flashy bright males only in breeding season (spring and summer), you're going to end up confused much of the rest of the year when the males get a lot duller.

The final issue is that colors are much more subtle in most groups of birds than in those I mention above. Most seabirds, shorebirds, raptors, and sparrows come in varying shades of brown, gray, black, and white that can take years to discern and truly understand. (You can get a head start, though, by jumping ahead to Chapter 21: Tackling Difficult Birds, Group by Group.) Which means you will have to start peeling back some of a bird's other attributes such as . . .

## Shape

As you saw, a bird's shape dominated my ID poll results, and it wasn't until I thought more about it that I truly appreciated its importance. Why is shape so revealing? It could be that our brains are just better at cataloging and storing shapes than sizes and colors. Another factor, however, is that size and color are often difficult to judge in the field.

My son likes to say, "It is possible to mistake almost any bird for almost any other bird." He's got a point. Often, birds are flitting around in the

tops of trees or scurrying in the brush where lighting conditions are less than ideal, rendering the bird's colors almost useless for identification. A backlit bird against a bright sky can pose the same problem, and in my birding career I have mistaken ravens for eagles, ducks for cormorants, buntings for bluebirds, and crossbills for House Finches.

Even in crummy conditions, however, shape gives us a reliable tool to narrow down possibilities. A few pages ago I mentioned the typical roundish, chubby shape of robins, which is shared by many different thrushes—and hard to confuse with other groups of birds. Woodpeckers, sparrows, gulls, and most other groups present their own unique silhouettes, both when flying and when perched.

What should you look for? A short list includes posture, tail length, bill shape, leg length, wing length, wing width, head shape, and body thickness—but you will learn that it depends on the birds. Here are just a few examples:

- A medium-sized bird with a large, heavy bill, poised at roughly a 45-degree angle from head to tail, might be a jay, magpie, crow, or other corvid.
- A smallish bird with a delicate, pointy bill and positioned horizontally will probably lead you to some kind of songbird such as a warbler or vireo.

- A medium to large roundish bird walking on the ground is probably a grouse, quail, or other game bird—unless it's in a marsh, in which case it may be some kind of rail.
- A small to medium bird with a short, triangular bill and fairly erect posture shouts "finch."
- A bird stooped over at the beach that is *not* a gull, well, you've got to think shorebird such as sandpiper, willet, godwit, or plover.
- Narrow, pointy wings and moving fast? Shorebird, falcon, dove, or pigeon.
- Standing erect on the side of a tree? Woodpecker, nuthatch, or creeper.

These examples merely scratch the surface. Other groups have their own "shapely" features, ones that you'll become adept at over time. My main point here is that shape gestalt will come to play a very important role in your identification repertoire, so it's a great thing to pay attention to with any bird sighting.

## Movement

The more you bird, the more you will develop an instinctive understanding for how particular species move, whether it's on the ground, in a tree, or in flight. As we've seen, robins live almost everywhere in the US, and they are fun to observe. On the ground, they tend to make short little sprints and then halt suddenly to eyeball the ground for prey. Magpies and crows, on the other hand, tend to hop from one place to another.

Flight patterns are even more revealing. Robins tend to flap several times, take a brief pause, and begin flapping again. Corvids tend to fly with fairly steady wingbeats. Woodpeckers often adopt a "flap-flap-glide" pattern, while sandpipers and many other shorebirds frantically flap hell-bent-for-leather, pausing only to make radical banked turns. Is it circling slowly above you, rarely flapping its wings? Then it's probably some kind of eagle, hawk, or vulture. To help you learn more about how birds move, ask yourself questions such as:

- Is that bird more inclined to walk, hop, or fly?
- How quickly does it move?
- Is it constantly pecking or digging for food, or does it take frequent breaks to look around?
- If it's on a tree trunk, is it walking up the tree or down?
- Does it have rapid wingbeats or fly slow and steady?
- If it's in tree branches, is it sitting still or busily flitting from one branch to the next, probing for food?
- If perched, does it "sally" out to snag insects from the air and then return to its perch, or wait to swoop down on prey on the ground?
- If it's high in the sky, is it flapping to get somewhere or circling slowly on broad wings?

As far as this last question, a large bird that is slowly circling suggests a vulture, eagle, or hawk. I recently accompanied renowned birder and author

Dan Casey to a hawk-watch location. Scientists and volunteers have established more than three hundred of these sites in North America and their mission is to count and identify migrating birds of prey. This particular site, located on a ridge

above Jewel Basin, Montana, especially attracts Cooper's Hawks and Sharp-shinned Hawks, two species that look extremely similar and are notoriously difficult to tell apart. I asked Dan how to distinguish them in flight, and he ticked off a number of features. The most useful thing he said was, "Since Sharp-shinned Hawks are a little smaller than Cooper's they tend to be tippier in the wind. Cooper's Hawks fly with more stability—like a larger sailboat compared to a smaller one." It's a nuance I probably could have learned only from another birder, and a valuable one to tuck into my ID library.

## Location

One final critical bird ID feature I want to discuss is *where* you happen to be birding, as well as when. I broach it last not because it is less important than others, but because most people incorporate it naturally. One time, my son and I were in Monterey, California, and we spotted a night-heron in a tree next to the parking lot. Without hesitation, Braden exclaimed, "Black-crowned Night-Heron!" Not being well-versed in night-herons, I asked, "How do you know that's a Black-crowned and not a Yellow-crowned?" He regarded me patiently. "Because Yellow-crowned Night-Herons don't live in California."

D'oh.

That experience imparted an indelible lesson: *different birds live in different places* and at different times of the year. This is true both on large geographic scales and smaller local habitat scales. The best way to rule out possible birds is to learn which species do and do not live in the place and habitat where you happen to be. Sure, an occasional vagrant (a bird way out of its normal range) may show up, but observing local birds and studying range maps in your field guide may be the best ways to sharpen your ID skills. I will trust you to know the part of the country you happen to be in, but here are some of the main habitat types you will encounter and want to take note of, keeping in mind that most birds are incredibly picky about which ones they choose to live in:

- **Conifer forests:** tall trees with cones such as pine, fir, and spruce

- **Deciduous forests:** trees that lose their leaves every year such as maple, beech, and elm
- **Riparian zones:** habitats bordering streams, rivers, ponds, and lakes
- **Grasslands:** these can be short or tall and include meadows, prairie, and cattle pastures
- **Sagebrush:** can be short or tall and occupy huge swaths of Western states
- **Mountains:** these can be covered with trees, grass, or scrub depending on geographic location and altitude
- **Shore:** everything from sandy beaches to rocky shores
- **Mangroves:** mainly limited to southern Florida

I'll go into much greater detail about habitats and the birds they contain in Chapter 13: Habitat Hopping.

## Bringing It All Together

Other features will accumulate on your "to learn" list as you dive deeper into identification, and especially for those of us past our prime learning years, these can feel overwhelming. Don't panic. Older brains are much better at learning than you might think. The more you get out there, the more your gray matter will pull it all together.

Not long ago, I asked University of Montana ornithologist—and fellow Boomer—Dick Hutto to meet me to discuss bird identification. We were sitting on a sunny bench overlooking the Clark Fork River, surrounded by shrubs filled with birds. I had invited Hutto specifically to talk about the challenges of identifying bird vocalizations—a topic I'll explore in the next chapter—but while we sat there, a bird flew by in our peripheral vision, and Hutto gave me an important insight into how we birders integrate information.

"So when it comes to identifying birds," he told me, "I suspect a lot of what people are using are things that they're not even talking about—that you won't find in the field guides. Like we just saw a bird fly in there? It was a chickadee. How did I know? I mean, I didn't see enough to go to a field guide and look at the characteristics. But the bird was little. It had a bounce when it flew. And we're in a riparian zone, so what else could it be? A lot of bird identification comes from experience being outside. The more you're out, the more you tally up all the possibilities, and eventually you know what's possible and it doesn't take as much to identify it. And that's bird-watching."

More often than not, you won't identify a new bird in the field your first time—or perhaps even the tenth or twelfth time. But every encounter helps you amass more details both consciously and subconsciously, improving your chances of a correct ID the next time. The goal is to embrace not just the result but the process. In birding, *struggle is the key to success*—and a big part of what makes birding so much fun. On every outing you get to solve mysteries, and having that mindset even with common birds will allow you to notice, learn, and enjoy more details about every species you encounter.

## CHAPTER 7

# Sounding Out Birdsong

One may argue that the "Getting Started" section of this book may not be the best place to introduce birdsong since "ear birding," or learning to identify birds by their vocalizations, is often considered an advanced topic. This can be especially true for Boomers and other people with compromised hearing. On the other hand, some beginning birders have a natural affinity for bird sounds and quickly start to pick them up. Furthermore, if you have any hearing left at all, birdsong will *eventually* become one of your most valuable bird identification tools. To wit, many ornithologists use it almost exclusively to identify species, particularly in forests and grasslands where birds are hard to see. It is so important, and so different from identifying birds visually, that many authors have written entire books about the subject. For now, if you'd like to skip this chapter and come back to it later, be my guest, but if bird vocalizations already tickle your curiosity, listen up!

## Songs vs. Calls

One of the first things to know about bird sounds is that *songs* and *calls* are not the same things, despite popular, casual use of both terms to refer to all bird vocalizations. *Songs* are often melodious and are the vocalizations most of us associate with birds. Songs are almost exclusively used by males to attract mates and advertise or defend their territories.

Most birds, however, also have a great repertoire of *calls*. Calls consist of chips, clicks, tseeps (yes, an official bird call descriptor), and other shorter, less sexy sounds birds employ to keep in contact with each other, issue warnings, and for purposes that no doubt elude us mere humans. The *chicka-dee-dee-dee* of the chickadee is perhaps the most easily recognized bird call, but most are not nearly so intelligible or helpful in identifying birds when you're just starting out. Because of that, I'll focus the discussion here on songs, beginning with what they are composed of.

## Dissecting Birdsong

Bruce Byers is an associate professor of biology at the University of Massachusetts, Amherst and has been studying and teaching bird vocalizations for more than three decades. "Almost all songbird songs consist of syllables," he explained to me a while back. "There are shorter bits of sound that are strung together to form songs, with very, very short bits of silence between them. Each bit is what we call a syllable or an element or something like that."

Even within a species, not all individuals have the same songs. Each male Lazuli Bunting, for instance, has its own unique song constructed from about 140 possible syllables. Birds of the same species also can sound quite different depending on the region in which they live, and the same bird can switch up its song with aggravating frequency. In one study of about forty male Chestnut-sided Warblers, for instance, Byers discovered that the birds totally replaced their songs over the course of a decade—but that the new songs still retained many of the same syllables as the old songs. Which offers a first big clue to learning: pay as much attention to the different syllables or elements of a song as to the overall sequence.

Some of the more common words used to describe songs include "cheerful," "harsh," "lilting," "buzzy," "rising," "falling," "squeaky," "melodic," "chattery," "bright," and "halting." The more you listen, the more you'll connect these words with what you are hearing. If you don't, well, choose your own adjectives! People with musical backgrounds seem to come up with especially useful birdsong descriptions, so if that's you, please jump in and expand our collective birdsong lexicon.

## Memorizing Mnemonics, Finding Feelings

A popular tool for learning bird vocalizations is mnemonics. Associating parts of a bird's song with words that you already know can make it easier to remember a song or song element the next time you hear it. I find mnemonics incredibly useful as long as I can hear a bird's complete song. A simple web search will yield comprehensive lists of common birdsong mnemonics, but some of the most popular include the following:

- *"Cheery-up. Cheery-up."* American Robin
- *"Who cooks for you?"* Barred Owl
- *"Fitz-pew."* Willow Flycatcher
- and my favorite, *"Quick-three-beers"* from the Olive-sided Flycatcher.

Many birders make up their own mnemonics that make sense to them, but it's not something I'm very good at. You'll probably do better.

A more right-brain strategy than mnemonics is to just focus on the "feel" of a song. Ornithologist Debbie Leick works for the private research and conservation facility MPG Ranch in Montana. Even though she studies the nocturnal flight calls of birds, she finds that learning birdsong still poses a challenge. "For me, learning a bird's song boils down to learning the tone and maybe some of the characteristics of how it sounds," she explains. "American Goldfinches and Lazuli Buntings are *bright*—and I don't even know what I mean by bright. It's just that they're really clear. And then the Lazuli Bunting's song to me is really bouncy. It has a bouncy characteristic to it, with a burry element at the end. So if you know things like that, even if the bird is switching up its song, you can still home in on it."

## Sonograms, Spectrograms, and Sound ID

Leick and many other experienced ornithologists find it extremely helpful to study bird sonograms, also called spectrograms. These are time-sequence graphs of a bird's song that show which frequencies it is producing, much akin to a musical score. Sonograms help scientists analyze what they are hearing by using that stronger, visual part of their brains for learning. Many online resources—including eBird, which I'll talk about in detail in Chapter 22: eBird: A Birder's Lifeline—provide sonograms of a bird's vocalizations. I personally don't find sonograms that useful for learning songs, but many birders do.

One thing I *do* find incredibly useful is a relatively new tool called Sound ID. I'll discuss other apps for learning songs later, but Sound ID is so useful that I have to talk about it now. **Sound ID** is part of the Cornell Lab of Ornithology's Merlin app and allows you to identify songs on the, ahem, fly. How does it work? Well, whenever you are out birding and you hear a song—or multiple songs—around you that you don't know, start Sound ID on your phone and the program begins spitting out IDs on your screen. The program was developed using AI (artificial intelligence) algorithms and, I gotta say, it just blows me away. It works almost in real time, requires no cell tower signal, and in my experience is about 90 percent accurate. Oh, and did I mention that it also displays the sonogram of what you are hearing?

All that said, I don't use Sound ID as the sole basis for identifying birds. If I think I hear a song that I know, but am not sure, I'll use the app to confirm the ID. More often, I run Sound ID to alert me to which birds might be in the area. Especially with my crummy ears, I often don't even detect a lot of calls, but if a Pine Siskin or Nashville Warbler pops up on Sound ID, then it helps me know what to look for.

## Birdsong Learning Apps and Online Learning Tools

Before wrapping up this chapter, I'd be remiss if I didn't point out some fun apps designed to help you learn at your own pace. For those just starting, **Chirp! Bird Songs & Calls USA** is a little app that offers quizzes from a library of several hundred bird vocalizations. It also allows you to build your own quiz of, say, wrens to help you get proficient at particular groups.

**Larkwire** takes quizzing to the next level, testing you on categories of calls such as Clear-toned Songs, Simple Songs, and Rattles & Trills. Built on a freemium model, you can pay for additional modules as your skills increase.

Other apps, such as the **Audubon Owls Guide**, also offer quizzing on bird vocalizations. Just how well apps will help you learn songs and calls depends on your own particular ears, brain, and patience, but if learning to bird by ear is important to you, I recommend trying these out. I also should mention a couple of online resources from Cornell. One is the **Bird Song Hero** game, a short introduction to birdsong ID that you can do with the young people in your life. It's also a nice way to start learning about bird sonograms or spectrograms.

The other is **eBird**. Again, I will discuss eBird in greater detail later, but the web version's vast array of tools includes both photographic and birdsong quizzes that are randomly generated by the region and time of year that interest you. I use these a lot when preparing to bird in a new location and, to be honest, find them more helpful than the apps above.

As with anything, learning songs takes *patience and practice*, especially for an older brain. Try several different strategies to see if one or two work for you. If, like me, you just don't seem to get it, don't beat yourself up. For many of us, learning vocalizations may not be in the cards—but don't let that stop you from enjoying birds in other ways.

When I asked Byers if there are other reasons we have trouble learning them, he elaborated, "I think the big reason is just the biases in the human sensory system. I think we're just really visual creatures, much more than our other senses. The other thing is that bird songs seem to happen fast. I don't know if it's a limitation of our brain or a limitation of our ears, but one thing that I do in my ornithology class is play songs down to half speed or a quarter speed so students can hear the detail a lot better."

## CHAPTER 8

# Feeders, Houses, and Water Features: A Great Way to Begin

To wrap up this section on getting started, I want to introduce an activity that can rapidly advance your birding skills and knowledge: installing bird feeders, birdhouses, and water features. Not all of us have yards to do this, but these items can also be set up in windows and on small porches and patios—even in common areas if it's not against the rules. Many parks and nature centers also set up bird feeders, houses, and water features, and encourage the public to drop by and take a look. If you have the time and energy to do this, you'll probably be amazed at the variety of birds that visit. Let's start with the most popular item to install: feeders.

## To Feed or Not to Feed?

Before installing a bird feeder, be aware that there has been some controversy among scientists and the birding community about feeding birds. On the "pro" side, feeders can be an important source of supplemental food for local birds, especially during lean winter or summer months, and during the breeding season when bird parents can't afford to buy their ravenous chicks the jumbo bags of Goldfish that nourish so many American children. On the "con" side, feeders can attract pests, make birds dependent on artificial sources of food, and most devastatingly, contribute to the spread of diseases such as botulism, salmonellosis, and avian pox. In between these two extremes, quite a few birders consider feeding birds a neutral exercise, one that neither benefits nor harms wild populations— but does provide enjoyment to people.

What to do?

As in all matters, I prefer to go with cautious common sense. I've read compelling arguments, for instance, against both tube feeders and platform-type feeders. One recent article provided strong, albeit nonscientific, evidence that tube feeders are especially prone to spreading *Mycoplasma* bacteria that can blind and kill finches. Even frequently disinfecting these feeders does not solve the problem because birds constantly rub their eyes and faces against the open ports that dispense the seeds, and this recontaminates the feeders. Meanwhile, other experts warn against platform feeders because sick birds can trample across food, infecting it and spoiling it with feces. Food on platform feeders is also open to the elements and at greater risk from spoilage.

While not the results of rigorous studies, the above arguments seem logical enough for me to avoid these two types of feeders. When properly cleaned and maintained, however, other types of feeders seem to pose minimal threat to birds. So, at least at this time, this compels me to say, "If you're so inclined, go ahead and give it a whirl." You may be helping birds, and there's no doubt you will learn a lot. Before taking this step, though, do your own research, read through the recommendations on the following pages, and carefully assess your space and your own habits around cleanliness.

"What about hummingbird feeders?" you may ask. Many people love to put out hummingbird feeders and delight in the tiny birds they attract. Thousands of feeders, along with extensive plantings of exotic flowering plants, may be partly responsible for huge range extensions of Anna's Hummingbird along the West Coast and the increase of Ruby-throated Hummingbirds that skip migration and overwinter in the Southeast. Even so, I don't put up hummingbird feeders myself. I am too lazy to

mix the sugary liquid and consistently replace it so that it doesn't spoil. I've also observed that drippings from the feeders can make a big mess that attracts yellow jackets, ants, and other pests. Most important, hummingbirds live on such razor-thin caloric margins that if I somehow forgot to refill a feeder, it could mean death for a hummingbird that has come to depend on it.

## Backyard Bird University

If you do decide you'd like to try feeding birds, you'll quickly discover that bird feeders come in a remarkable variety of shapes and sizes, and attract different kinds of birds. You can choose from hopper-type feeders, thistle feeders, suet feeders, oriole (fruit) feeders, hummingbird feeders, and so many more that I won't even attempt a comprehensive survey here. Braden and I hang small general-purpose hopper-style feeders that contain a simple, covered compartment for holding birdseed and two small dispenser trays along the bottom. As birds remove the seeds, more seeds flow down into the trays, and the clear plexiglass walls of the compartment tell us when the hopper needs to be refilled.

Besides putting up feeders, adding a water feature to your yard can be an excellent way to attract birds and learn to identify them. A dependable water supply can prove critical to birds in many areas. An ideal water feature fills itself, is shallow so that birds can bathe in it, and has plenty of perching spots that birds can use to get a drink. Water features also, of course, need to be cleaned regularly.

No matter where you live, you will probably be surprised by the variety of bird species that visit your feeders and water features. At our house, we are fortunate to back up to a small area of ponderosa pines that, in turn, sits only a quarter mile or so from a wild creek. Since we began

birding, Braden and I have sighted sixty-seven species in or near our yard. Many are specifically attracted to the feeders, but while we're watching the feeders we spot many other species—especially migrating birds that are skulking around as they pass through to somewhere else. Directly and indirectly, the feeders have allowed us close-up looks that have taught us how to identify many of these local birds.

I'll just come out and say this: Don't put up a feeder or water feature if you're not willing to keep it as clean and disease-free as possible. Various experts recommend the following steps to reduce the risk of spreading avian diseases at feeders:

- Install multiple feeders if you have space to do so. This spreads out birds so they are less prone to come into close contact and transmit disease.
- Thoroughly disinfect and scrub feeders with a mixture of one part bleach to nine parts water. This should be done every 1 to 4 weeks depending on how many birds are using the feeder and other factors.
- Place feeders at least fifteen feet or so from vegetation to reduce the risk of sneak attacks by predators.

# Birdhouses

Birdhouses, more properly called nesting boxes, can be a great addition to your yard and bird-watching experience—again, if you know what you're doing. Most cavity-nesting birds—those that naturally nest in holes—are *extremely* particular about the kind of place they want to nest. They want boxes that are a certain size and shape, and with just the right size of entry hole. Notable exceptions include House Sparrows and European Starlings, two species you definitely *don't* want moving into your yard, but will take up residence in almost anything.

A quick internet search will tell you which entry-hole sizes the various cavity-nesting birds prefer. The only boxes we put up have holes that are 1⅛ to 1¼ inches in diameter—the size that is just right for chickadees, House Wrens, and nuthatches. Anything larger, including the always-popular

bluebird nest boxes, will allow House Sparrows to move in—as will the ridiculous birdhouses built to look like mansions, barns, castles, and so forth that you find at many hardware and garden supply stores. Unless you are willing to constantly monitor your bluebird box (or ornamental box) and evict unwanted intruders, I wouldn't mess with one. Instead, stick to a basic box made with untreated wood that targets the specific kinds of birds you want to attract. Also, don't buy boxes with little perching pegs under the entry holes. Native birds don't need 'em, and pegs might help attract House Sparrows or other unwanted tenants.

I've found it surprisingly difficult to locate boxes with 1⅛-inch openings. The Wild Birds Unlimited franchise does carry some, or if you're crafty at all, the boxes aren't difficult to make, and you can easily download a set of plans. What to do if your boxes have holes that are too big and you want to allow only smaller birds inside? An easy solution is to buy metal or wooden guards with holes of smaller diameter, and just screw them on over your present hole. Do a search on "birdhouse guard" or "birdhouse predator guard" and a whole variety of different sizes will pop up.

In addition to being picky about hole sizes, birds pay attention to how far off the ground a birdhouse is located, which direction it's facing, and what kind of vegetation is nearby. House Wrens, for instance, like a house six to ten feet above the ground while chickadees prefer a couple feet lower, and both seem to like a nearby bush or two to help them stealthily approach the box. I try to make sure our birdhouses face away from the afternoon sun and receive some shade so the babies won't get cooked, but bird preferences vary. Most birdhouses come with instructions about all of this, but if not, be sure you do some research before installation.

- To prevent bird food from spoiling, use smaller feeders that need to be refilled regularly.
- Clean up spilled seed and bird droppings under the feeder often.

Seed feeders—as with hummingbird feeders—also should be kept full in case any birds are depending on them. This is especially true during breeding seasons and extreme weather conditions, and applies equally to water features in warmer weather.

## Unwanted Intruders

Whatever "birdy" features you install, it's an excellent bet that not all of your avian visitors will be welcome. House Sparrows and European Starlings in particular are exotic, invasive, nuisance birds that often bully native species and even kill their chicks. One way to dissuade nuisance birds is by putting only black oil sunflower seeds in your feeders, rather than the commercial birdseed mixes that often contain low-quality millet and other seeds that invasive species love. House Sparrows and starlings *will* eat black oil sunflower seeds but, from what I've observed, not as ravenously. This allows native birds to better compete. Another way to deal with these invasives is to trap and, yes, kill them (see Chapter 29: The Bird-Friendly Yard).

Birds don't have to be exotic to be pests, however. Native jays, grackles, and other species can overrun a feeder, shoving aside other birds you also want to see. There's not a lot you can do about this, so you'll have to perform your own calculations on whether you want to keep feeding these bossy birds. A similar argument can be applied to rats and squirrels, but with these there are a number of shields, squirrel baffles, and other exclusion devices that can potentially keep these pesky mammals from copping a free meal.

If you decide to add feeders or water features to your yard, be aware that an abundance of birds often attracts cats and other predators. These predators fall into two categories: avian and furry. Many bird lovers are shocked to see Cooper's and Sharp-shinned Hawks picking off songbirds at their feeders. Again, there's not a lot you can do about this, so you have to decide whether the thrill of watching a hawk snatch a cardinal or chickadee off your feeder is worth the guilt you feel about serving up the poor innocent victim in the first place. I like hawks, so it would depend on which species they are eating. If they're picking off House Sparrows and starlings, I'm all for it!

Cats are a different matter. The few scientific studies that have been done suggest that outdoor and feral cats are responsible for killing hundreds of millions of songbirds every year—maybe more. Additional, rigorous research is needed, but it is evident that cats make a significant impact on birds and may be directly leading to the decline of many bird populations. I have noticed cats staking out our own backyard feeders dozens of times. Our dog Lola solved this problem, driving away any curious felines, but if you don't have a "cat dog," try to place your feeders and water features where cats can't reach them—or perhaps opt not to install them in the first place. I'll discuss cats in greater detail in Chapter 30: Keeping Cats Indoors.

# PART III

# BEING PREPARED: WHAT ELSE YOU'LL NEED

*There are no secrets to successful birding. It is the result of preparation, lots of phone apps, and really bitchin' clothes.*
*—Colin Powell*

## CHAPTER 9

# Field Guide Apps and Avian Websites

I was planning to wait until a later chapter to discuss *all* birding-related apps, but since smartphones are dribbling into this book in other locations, let's take a more comprehensive look at some of them now. One app I'm going to wait on is eBird. Many birders find both the app and web version of this amazing program to be one of our most important tools, and

if you'd like to skip ahead to the eBird chapter, go for it (Chapter 22). For a beginner, however, eBird can be a tad overwhelming, so for now, let's focus on field guide apps and websites that might be especially useful.

### Field Guide Apps

As I pointed out in Chapter 5: The Birding Field Guide, I love physical bird field guides, and Braden and I used to religiously haul a bound copy of one with us on even the longest birding hikes. As we have become more proficient at bird identification, however, we have opted for birding guide apps more and more. While not as easy on the eyes as a bound book, the apps make up for this by reducing chiropractor visits and, often, by providing cool additional features such as:

- Sample audio of vocalizations for each species
- Suggestions of places to bird near you
- Keeping lists of what you see

The Cornell Lab of Ornithology's **Merlin** app (which contains Sound ID) is the best place to start. Merlin provides a full field guide to species occurring in the ABA Area (North America north of Mexico plus the Hawaiian Islands) and helps you ID birds using physical features, photos, and sounds. It allows you to record your bird sightings directly with Merlin or, as I recommend, it can also connect you to eBird to do so. Merlin can even figure out which birds might be near you. Best of all Merlin is *free*, which I'm sure has generated a lot of cursing and death threats from other app makers, especially because Merlin is so good.

While you're checking out free birding apps, download **The Audubon Bird Guide**. This excellent app offers great field guide content, including a bit more detail than Merlin about each bird's ecology and conservation status. An especially nice feature lets you view recent sightings of species near your current location. It also hooks up with eBird to show birding hotspots near you. Both Merlin and the Audubon app have tools to help you ID birds by shape, size, color, and more. You can also record your bird sightings on the Audubon app—though, as with Merlin, I recommend using eBird for this since it has become the dominant player in the data collection game.

But take heart, capitalists! Birders can actually *buy* birding apps, too! The one Braden and I have ended up using the most is **Sibley Birds**. Like its hardbound cousin, the Sibley app provides a wonderful field guide with illustrations, descriptions, maps, and more. The *main* reason I go to it is its uber-cool feature that allows me to compare two species side by side. I can't tell you how many times I have used this in the field when trying to fathom the differences between, say, a Semipalmated or a Western Sandpiper. I'll go so far as to say that this feature alone makes it worth contributing to David Sibley's retirement fund.

**The iBird Pro Guide to Birds** is another popular birding app available for purchase that includes the birds of North America (including Hawai'i), the UK and Ireland, and Palau. If you're a warbler fanatic, you might also consider **The Warbler Guide**, a fun app that helps you with almost every conceivable aspect of warbler identification, including illustrations of the birds from underneath—a frustratingly common view.

## Avian Websites

This is a shocking fact, but not all useful avian material is available on apps! Other great bird and birding material still resides on that Stone Age technology known as "the website." Websites have incredible information for both beginning and advanced birders. Below are some of my favorites, along with a couple of others, to give you an idea of what's out there. Conduct your own web searches and you'll find many, many more.

**Audubon Bird Migration Explorer** (explorer.audubon.org) is an incredible website that shows detailed migration routes of more than 450 species of birds, including the actual tracks taken by individuals tagged with geolocator and other tracking devices. This site was built with the collaboration of many heavy hitters in the birding world, and I gotta say it blew me away. Fair warning: you could spend much of the rest of your life exploring it, so be careful!

# Banding Codes

One common feature of many birding apps and programs is providing you with several ways to record or locate a bird on a list. Most allow you to type in the bird's common name, its scientific name, or its four-letter banding code. For those not familiar with banding codes, this last option deserves some explanation.

Banding codes are basically shortcuts developed by scientists to simplify their task of recording bird names. Banding codes generally come in two types. From what I hear, scientists in Latin America favor six-letter codes based on a bird's scientific name, but here in the good ole United States, birders and banding organizations generally rely on four-letter codes based on bird common names. Four-letter banding codes *usually* consist of the first two letters of a bird's first name followed by the first two letters of its second name. For instance, the banding code for American Robin is AMRO. The one for Mountain Bluebird is MOBL. For Brown Pelican it's BRPE and so forth.

Unfortunately, not all bird common names fit into this scheme, but outliers generally follow a common-sense strategy. Black-capped Chickadee, for instance, is BCCH. Killdeer is KILL. Northern Rough-winged Swallow is NRWS. You get the idea.

Occasionally, you'll encounter clashes between two birds that could have the same banding code. What then? Usually, the more common bird gets the more straightforward code. Barrow's Goldeneye, for instance, keeps BAGO while Barnacle Goose gets saddled with BRNG, which unfairly suggests that the bird is "boring."

To complicate matters further, different birding organizations have developed slightly different sets of codes. That said, banding codes are fun and you'll quickly get the hang of them. To learn more, simply do a web search for "four-letter bird banding codes" and you will find several excellent articles on the subject.

Speaking of Audubon, I should mention that they have a wonderful, free version of their **Audubon Bird Guide** at audubon.org/bird-guide. It's perfect for beginners and is a great way to get some quick information about a species, its biology, and distribution.

**All About Birds** (allaboutbirds.org) is the Cornell Lab of Ornithology's version of a free online bird guide. If you can't find your bird in the Audubon guide, you'll probably find it here.

For those who want to delve deeper into a species, another amazing product from Cornell is their **Birds of the World** site (birdsoftheworld.org). This provides detailed information on thousands of ABA Area *and* international species. For each species, the latest scientific findings are given for almost every aspect of the bird's biology. The full version requires an annual fee, but I use this site almost daily and find it well worth the money.

**Fatbirder** (fatbirder.com) bills itself as "the premier birders' web resource about birds, birding and birdwatching." I can't swear that this is true, but I admire the boldness of the claim, and the site does burst with information. This includes, but is not limited to, species information, equipment reviews, travel tips, and much, much more. Launched by Bo Beolens out of Great Britain, Fatbirder has a more international focus than many sites you'll run into—something that makes it particularly useful to the international bird explorer.

With a similar homegrown feel as Fatbirder, **Bird Watching HQ** (bird watchinghq.com) offers a wealth of information about birds and how to attract them to your yard. It's a good place to go for reviews of feeders, equipment, and more.

Look around the web, and you will find many more excellent—and not so excellent—sources of bird fun and information.

## CHAPTER 10

# Birding Action Wear

Now that we've covered both the essential, and perhaps less essential, tools you'll need to get started birding, we can *finally* enter what everyone will agree is the most thrilling topic of this book: what to wear.

Don't worry. In keeping with the timeless intent of this guide, I will refrain from giving an in-depth review of trendy clothing designers and brand recommendations, but I still think it's worth holding brief discussions about basic birding attire. As you might expect, these focus on the three fundamental apparel attributes: comfort, utility, and making other birders insanely jealous.

Picking out what you're going to wear while birding largely depends on what kind of birding you plan to do. If you are going to be mostly driving around in a car, well honestly, I don't care what you wear. Want to don your Captain Kirk starship casuals? Go for it. Most of the time, however, we birders will make at least short and medium excursions outside of a vehicle, so we need to dress accordingly.

If you live in almost any temperate part of the world, it's good advice to follow the basic outdoor mantra of dressing in layers. Here in Montana, it can be sunny one minute and hailing the next, so I want to make sure I'm prepared for such dramatic shifts—at least enough so that I can make it back to the car alive. If Braden and I, for instance, are going to be walking or hiking for a couple of miles, I'll pack at least a sweatshirt, and in most months, some kind of light rain jacket as well. Keep in mind that wool will keep you warmer than cotton when you do get caught out in a rainstorm or blizzard.

But let me get the marbles out of my mouth and focus on birding wear, item by item.

## Hat

Ever since I was a Boy Scout, I have considered a hat an essential outdoor item whether or not I am birding, and you should too. Wide-brimmed hats make the most sense in most situations because of the protection they provide to your face and neck. They also allow you to carry more water in them if you need to douse a forest fire—and yes, this has happened to me! Plus, let's face it, wide-brimmed hats also look really bitchin' and let you show off your personality.

Nonetheless, I stick to the basic baseball cap when I'm birding. Why? Because a wide-brimmed hat blocks your view of birds overhead and can distort bird calls—a troublesome issue for people like me who wear hearing aids. Additionally, I own so many baseball-type caps that they allow me to express my every mood and whim. If I'm feeling especially virtuous, I might wear my Cornell Lab of Ornithology hat. If I want to identify with my Southern roots, I'll wear my Bob's BBQ cap. If I want to contribute to academic tribalism, I'll wear my Cal Golden Bears cap. Whatever I choose, I make sure to add sunscreen to my ears to block the extra UV exposure.

## Shirt

For most of my birding life, I have worn T-shirts while birding. Not only are they comfortable, but they excel at provoking envy from other birders. My favorite used to be the one I bought while birding High Island, Texas, with Braden. Wearing it, I could almost hear other birders whisper, "Wow, he's been to High Island? He is *so* cool." When that shirt eventually dissolved, I switched to one from Ohio's Black Swamp Bird Observatory, home of the self-proclaimed "Biggest Week of Birding"—though I never admit that I haven't yet birded there.

Despite my love of T-shirts, many veteran birders I meet wear collared and long-sleeved "technical" shirts designed to breathe, and in fact, I have started to wear these myself—especially when birding in Texas, Florida, and other semitropical areas. Not only do these shirts dissuade biting insects, their UPF fabrics protect my already eroding epidermis. Sure, I sweat a bit more, but not having to totally encase myself in sunscreen and bug spray is worth the tradeoff.

Such shirts hold the added advantage of having extra pockets to hold things—and of looking dressier if you meet King Charles while out birding and he invites you back to Buckingham Palace for bangers and mash.

## Pants

Why anyone wears anything *other* than cargo pants is totally beyond me, but cargos have been my constant companions for the past fifteen years. I prefer styles with a built-in belt and elastic waistband, but it's the *hundreds of pockets* that render cargo pants hands down the best clothing invention since the leopard-skin wrap-around. You also won't find a pair of regular pants more comfortable. The one problem? The price. Go to a trendy sporting goods store and you can pay a day's wages or more for a pair. Big box stores, though, often have them for considerably less, and when they do, I stock up.

I do occasionally wear other pants. On warm, dry days when I know I'll be home before nightfall I'll rock a pair of shorts, and in winter I opt for the combo of sweats under a light pair of ski pants. While I miss all the pockets of cargo pants, this dynamic duo keeps me warm and comfy, especially when slogging long distances through the snow.

And speaking of slogging . . .

## Footwear

Despite the detailed discussions above, your footwear may be the most critical apparel choice you make as a birder. Braden and I very rarely wear anything but light hiking boots while birding, even if we are cruising New York's Central Park. They are acceptably comfortable and sturdy and allow us to navigate almost any obstacle, whether that's scrambling up a scree slope for a better look at a flying Peregrine or accidentally stepping in dog poop in the aforementioned park.

If you don't like boots, most hiking/walking shoes have these same attributes. Unfortunately, very few brands fit my large, weirdly shaped feet, but for those of you with feet solidly under the bell curve, you'll have many to choose from. Oh, and if you have my kind of feet, try Keen footwear or Skechers.

The only time we banish our boots is in winter or when we're navigating some kind of wetland. Then, we swap out hiking boots for cheap rubber-and-neoprene rain boots and two or three pairs of socks. These allow us to trudge through snow or keep our feet dry when we inevitably slip into freezing water while crossing an irrigation ditch, as we did when chasing our lifer Northern Hawk Owl. If you're shopping for a pair of rubber boots, try to find some with insoles that have a fairly thick insulating layer. These will keep your feet *much* warmer. For obvious reasons, it's a great idea to keep extra dry socks in the car or in your backpack. Warning: the soles of rubber boots often wear out quickly, but I've found that I can extend their lifetimes by layering shoe glue on the heels, especially if I wear the boots only in snow.

## Sunglasses and Goggles

Sunglasses, of course, add infinite bling to your birding outfit. Alas, you'll probably find that you won't wear sunglasses that much while birding because they get in the way of your binoculars. It's still a good idea to carry a pair, though, because you never know when you'll find yourself birding blindingly bright snow-covered slopes, beaches, or other infuriatingly dazzling landscapes. For more on using binoculars while wearing glasses, see Chapter 18: Physical Limitations II: Eyesight Issues.

A birding innovation that I'm exceedingly proud of is using ski goggles. I used to wear these only once a year when I got up my courage to go skiing, but I've learned to wear them on brutally cold birding days too. Not only do they keep my eyes warm in subzero temperatures, they allow me to withstand blasts of Arctic winds and ice without crying out like a two-year-old who has lost his binky. Try it the next time you're birding during a January cold front.

ALL OF THE above are just my own recommendations. With some trial and error, you'll discover the wardrobe that best suits your birding habits and fashion sense. One final suggestion is to dress in drabber, even camo, colors since bright colors tend to scare away some birds. The exception is during hunting season, when a bright orange vest and hat will distinguish you from an eight-point buck! Another piece of advice? Err on the side of warmth. If you're too warm you can always tie an extra raincoat or sweatshirt around your waist, but you can't pluck one from a nearby tree branch when you teeter on the verge of hypothermia.

Similarly, never forget your ski cap and gloves in winter or even in chilly fall and spring conditions. After all, it's really embarrassing to be chasing a flock of Pine Grosbeaks and have to be rescued by a Saint Bernard!

## CHAPTER 11

# The Avian Survival Kit

As indicated in the previous chapter, survival is a highly desirable outcome of any birding adventure, and in this regard I have one recommendation: Always bird with a paramedic. It's just unbelievable what these people carry around! Need a splint? Anticoagulation powder? Defibrillator? Enough bandages to fix up the Light Brigade after the Battle of Balaclava? Paramedics will fix you up.

Sadly, birding doesn't yet rank as the number-one hobby of paramedics, so you will probably need to make provisions for your own safety. If you plan to be birding a lot, in fact, I highly recommend taking wilderness-survival, first-aid, and CPR classes.

Whether or not you do that, water and food should accompany you on any birding excursion. Sure, if you're just going to roll or stroll fifty yards to an overlook to check for White-throated Swifts, you can probably leave your water bottle and snacks in the car. More often than not, however, even a short fifty-yard stroll turns into a much longer trek when you spot a mixed flock of warblers moving away from you, so you might want to be safer than sorrier. It's a great idea to always shove a couple of granola bars into your pockets no matter what your birding intentions may be.

Here are other safety items I suggest for longer hikes, especially if you plan on chasing a Rufous-vented Ground-Cuckoo off-trail:

- A first-aid kit containing, typically, various sizes of bandages, butterfly closure strips, ibuprofen, hard candy or cough drops, antihistamines, antacids (especially something to treat nausea or indigestion, which comes in handy for food- and waterborne ailments), antibiotic ointment, salt tablets, sterile wipes, medical tape, forceps, duct tape, and a couple rolls of gauze for wrapping wounds. Many companies make such kits, so you can shop according to your preference—or, better yet, put one together yourself.

- Specialized medicines or life-saving devices for your particular medical conditions (e.g., Epi-pen for an extreme allergic reaction)
- Headlamp with extra batteries

- Smartphone with extra recharging unit
- Multitool pocketknife
- Small roll of toilet paper in a resealable bag
- Sunscreen and lip balm
- Insect repellent
- Compass (a real one in case your phone dies) and map
- Matches and a lighter in a resealable bag
- Compact water filter
- Extra *non-cotton* socks to change into when your blisters have popped and oozed all over your feet. (For those who haven't compared cotton with wool or synthetic socks, cotton tends to absorb more sweat and water, which increases friction against your skin and creates more blisters.)
- A whistle to alert others in case of emergency—or when you happen to spot a Wandering Albatross several thousand miles from its normal range.

Of course, what you bring depends heavily on your particular birding plans. In areas where bears are common, for example, you may want to carry bear spray. Before you head out, invest a few minutes in thinking about where you are going, how long you will be out, and what misadventures might possibly greet you.

Oh yeah, and always tell someone *not with you* where you are going and when you'll be back so they can start dividing up your stuff when you fail to return.

# PART IV

# HITTIN' THE BIRDING TRAIL: WHERE TO GO

*I needed to go . . . the pull of birds was stronger*
*for me than any force on Earth.*
*—Tenzing Norgay*

## CHAPTER 12

# Local Explorations

Now that you're comfortably attired, suitably equipped, and aren't going to die—at least not from starvation, mosquito bites, or exposure—it's time to get out there and cash in those hours of preparation. In other words, it's time to go birding!

As enthralled as you might be with your backyard birds, it's a safe bet that soon you are going to want to start exploring the endless birding possibilities outside of your home habitat. If you've been a lot more successful saving for retirement than I have, you can begin your birding career by booking a guided ten-day luxury birding tour to South Africa or the Amazon—but I don't recommend it. Without some basic knowledge of birds, your trip will consist of a guide telling you, "There's a Horn-breasted Hippo-Pecker," and you replying, "Uh-huh. That's really cool." You will come home remembering only three species and feeling not very much smarter than when you left.

## Birding the Neighborhood

No matter where you live, there are cool birds to spot, enjoy, and identify, so I recommend you start birding at places within easy reach. Birding local is not only time efficient, it has the extra advantage of being free or at least inexpensive, again demonstrating that this activity can and should be enjoyed by anyone, no matter your situation. Where should you go?

Consider anywhere near you that has some decent habitat. Head to places with an assortment of bushes, trees, or water that aren't covered in asphalt (you'll learn a lot more about this in the next chapter, Chapter 13: Habitat Hopping). Even an overly manicured park is likely to have a few bird species tolerant of humans and our infrastructure, and getting good at identifying common birds such as robins, jays, crows, grackles, pigeons, doves, and House Sparrows will help build your birding foundations. A more natural area, though, will undoubtedly offer more variety.

You probably know of some natural areas nearby, but if not, try doing a web search on "Birding spots in (fill in your town)" or look up your local Audubon group's website. Local Audubon groups often post lists of good local birding sites, as well as details about how to bird there and what you might see. One thing I do, especially when I'm in a new place, is call up Google Maps and study any green spaces or trail systems that appear. If you have limited mobility, look for places with paved walking or biking trails. I recently searched "handi-capped accessible trails Missoula" and was delivered to the All Trails (alltrails.com) website. I was pleased to see that it included quite a number of trails in my hometown that are also good birding locations. More on this in Chapter 19: Physical Limitations III: The Broken-Down Bod.

As we'll discuss later, eBird is an excellent resource for finding birding hotspots, but good birding doesn't have to occur at officially recognized hotspots, parks, or trails. Some of mine and Braden's most fun birding

# The Early Birder Gets the . . .

Various birds can be active at all times of the day, depending on the species, habitat, season, weather, and behavioral factors like mating, nesting, and migration. That means that theoretically, almost any time is a good time to bird. However, for most species, especially songbirds, dawn presents your best opportunity for a successful outing.

In early morning, birds are literally waking up, hungry, and ready to start their day. "The minute there's enough light to see—bam—the birds are detecting motion," explains Dick Hutto, University of Montana ornithologist. "The insects are freezing, so the birds can pick them off—tick-tick tick [imitating a bird prying through bark for insects]—relatively easily."

Conversely, once the day warms up and the insects are flying, it becomes more difficult for birds to hunt, and they often settle down into the trees where they're harder to see. In most cases, the major action has wrapped up by eleven or noon, and the worst hours for birding generally occur in the heart of the afternoon. That makes this a perfect time to take a siesta or mix some margaritas until things begin to pick up, albeit to a lesser extent, in the evening.

What if afternoon is all you've got? Do not despair. Raptors take advantage of thermal air currents throughout the day. Ducks and geese stay visible and (mostly) active wherever there is water, while many shorebirds follow the tides more than the alarm clock. The more you're out there, the more you'll start to see which birds are out when, what patterns they might follow, and how this changes over the course of a year.

adventures unfold when we just drive around looking for promising habitat. It might be an irrigation ditch with some bushes growing along it. It could be an old, overgrown railroad right-of-way. Cemeteries often have great birding, provided they haven't been groomed and sprayed to, ahem, death. So can "brown sites"—abandoned factories or other industrial facilities that have sat rusting away for years. Birds are opportunistic, and if they find food, shelter, and a place to nest, many of them will move in. Just make sure to get permission before venturing onto private property.

## Flocking Up

As you begin birding, you might consider joining up with others. People have vastly varying desires for company when they are out "twitching" (a British word for birding that I abhor but slides in nicely here). Some people prefer to bird by themselves or with a patient spouse or significant other who serves as driver, gas station attendant, therapist, and trip planner. Others love the social aspects of birding, going out in groups and sharing their experiences with fellow avian fanatics. I enjoy both individual and group birding, but will say that for a beginner, going out with other birders offers significant rewards.

You can greatly enhance the process of learning both regional birds and birding spots by getting involved with a local Audubon Society chapter. Chapters sponsor bird outings, lectures, and classes for free or at reasonable prices. Other than the obvious advantage of meeting like-minded people, the biggest boon to this kind of social birding is how it accelerates the learning process. I don't know why this is, but I learn far more—and far more quickly—from another person than I do from studying a field guide. It could be that when I'm out in the field struggling intensely with an ID, my brain just snaps up information more efficiently than if I am sitting at home with a hypothetical bird ID in a book or online. A more experienced birder, though, can zero in on and explain why this bird is Species A and not Species B much better than a field guide can.

If you don't have an active Audubon group in your area, you can seek out other social birding opportunities.

# Social Media Connections

Like me, you may feel ambivalent about, if not downright hostile toward, social media, but I have to admit that social media platforms offer incredible resources for the birding community. The Montana Birding Facebook page, for example, has been a great place for me to connect with other birders, find new places to bird, share ideas, or simply have a good laugh.

Facebook hosts an endless array of birding-oriented pages based on region, species, demographic, and more, so buckle up. If you're in the Pacific Northwest, you could join Pacific Northwest Birding, Birding Oregon, or Western Washington Birders. In Northern California take your pick of Nor Cal Birding, Birding California, or San Francisco Bay Area Birding Group. Hot for a particular type of bird? Try Raptor ID; Finches, Irruptions, and Mast Crops; Pelagics: Seabirds Birding Worldwide; or Cardinals, Owls & Eagles Fans. Want to ask the experts? Join the ABA's What's this Bird? page. And how about birders just like you? Try World Girl Birders, Feminist Bird Club regional pages, Birdability Birders, or Black AF in STEM. The pages and names may change with time, but the people and interests will always be out there for you.

Instagram and TikTok are great for photos, videos, memes, and connecting with other birders that share your sense of humor. You can follow bird experts, photographers, birding and conservation organizations, national parks, you name it.

Meetup lists general and specialized birding and outdoor groups across the country, or you can start one of your own! Join or create a local WhatsApp group to be notified about local outings or rare birds. You can even find birding trips listed on Airbnb Experiences!

Whatever platform you use, the point is to find your people online, expand your community, and get out birding.

Where I live, birding classes are offered by a natural history center, the local university, and sometimes individual experts. If you live in a town of any size, you will probably find several options to choose from. Get on the mailing lists of your local college extension programs, city and state parks, nature centers, museums, and bird supply stores that may offer classes or outings.

Audubon and other groups often offer one-day field trips that don't require as much of a commitment as a class. The advantage of a class, however, is that it helps you get to know other birders better and gives you a solid overview of the best birding hotspots in your area throughout an entire birding season. Don't be shy! If you meet someone who doesn't offend you with their personal hygiene or horrible sense of humor, swap phone numbers and set up your own birding excursions. After all, it's not just experts who can teach you things. Struggling over a bird with another novice can be a great way to advance your skills—especially if you start birding together. I was fortunate to be able to do this with my son, but anyone will do—as long as they are willing to get up early and embrace the ups and downs of the learning process.

There are, of course, other ways to broaden your birding network. If you go out solo birding regularly, chances are you will begin to run into the same people over and over—people who might also be looking for birding buddies. Joining birding groups online—whether that's through Facebook, Meetup, or a local program—can also put you in touch with birders, as well as alert you to upcoming events and uber-cool birds that happen to be passing through.

Soon, it won't be you asking the difference between a Ruby-crowned Kinglet and an Orange-crowned Warbler. Instead, you will be teaching that difference to other beginning birders!

**CHAPTER 13**

# Habitat Hopping

As you begin venturing into your neighborhood, town, and other surroundings, you'll quickly notice that the birds you see usually depends on the type of place—or the habitat—where you are birding. This relationship is one of the most fascinating aspects of birding, and will teach you not only about birds but also about natural landscapes that too many people ignore. The more you bird, the more you'll learn that in order to find Bird A you'll need to go here, while to see Bird B you'll need to visit that place over there.

We've already touched on habitats a bit in Chapter 6: Braving Bird Identification, but let's take a closer look at seven important habitats you're likely to encounter, and what you might generally find there.

### Wetlands

Wetlands—especially those with open, easily viewed water—are ideal for the beginning birder. Wetlands is a broad term that covers lakes, ponds, marshes, rivers, and almost any other place with water in it at least sometime during the year. These are great places to bird because on a typical day, most host a variety of larger birds that are easily seen, fun to watch, and relatively simple to identify.

Ducks frequent wetlands and are the ultimate "gateway birds" for beginning birders. If you grew up looking only at Mallards, you will be astonished by the variety of shapes, colors, and behaviors *other* ducks offer. The first time I saw the blazing-white head patch of a male Buf-flehead, I felt almost spellbound, and I still thrill to see Buf-fleheads today. I can honestly say the same

for Northern Pintails, Northern Shovelers, Barrow's Goldeneyes, American Wigeons, Harlequin Ducks—well, it's a long list.

Wetlands with good parking and wide boardwalks are almost custom-made for birders with mobility issues, and with a good pair of binoculars or a spotting scope (which we'll talk about in Chapter 23) you'll be able to study even those obstinate birds that prefer the far side of the pond.

As you watch the ducks (and swans and geese), don't ignore the birds surrounding you in the trees, bushes, and cattails near the water. Especially listen for the variety of calls to alert you to different species. During much of the year you could see a few herons and other tall wading birds lurking among the cattails, along with Song Sparrows. In spring and summer Red-winged and Yellow-headed Blackbirds, Marsh Wrens, Common Yellowthroats, and Gray Catbirds might abound. If you hear a loud whooping sound from across the water, you're probably listening to a Wilson's Snipe. A loud chugging sound like a plunger? Could be an American Bittern. Merlin's Sound ID feature will give you a better idea of the richness around you. Depending on where you live and the season, keep a special eye out for Northern Harriers and Short-eared Owls. These charismatic birds of prey often inhabit and hunt in marshy areas, flying low and slow over the ground, using their incredible hearing to locate small mammals and other prey.

### Conifer Forests

In winter, forests of pine, spruce, and other conifers, or "cone-bearing trees," can seem pretty dead bird-wise, but as you walk, listen for the *chicka-dee-dee-dee-dee* alarm calls of chickadees. These delightful birds can be found in many habitats and are often accompanied by other bird species in aggregations known as "mixed-species flocks." You might see various nuthatches, Brown Creepers, and woodpeckers hunting and foraging with chickadees, so always stop to take a close look. And keep glancing up in case a Great Horned Owl or other raptor sits silently watching you. If you don't spot one, the crows might, and whenever you happen to hear a bunch of crazed crows yakking off about something, be sure to investigate. They are often mobbing an owl or other bird of prey!

In spring, conifer forests come alive as a variety of warblers, orioles, grosbeaks, finches, vireos, tanagers, and other songbirds migrate through or come to these forests to breed. Birding among tall trees involves a lot of looking up, which can be hard on the neck, and the birds are often silhouetted against pale backgrounds, but don't get frustrated. Just pick one bird and focus on it until you get a good look. As in other places, tap into Sound ID to find out what may be surrounding you.

### Deciduous Forests

Almost everything I wrote about conifer forests also applies to deciduous forests—those that drop their leaves every year. Deciduous forests consist of trees such as maple, beech, oak, chestnut, aspen, and other

"broad-leafed" trees. They are the main forests you'll find in the midwestern and eastern part of the continent but can be found in many western and southern locations too. Deciduous forests in particular can host a remarkable diversity of songbirds during the spring and summer breeding season. That's because these forests produce an unreal abundance
of caterpillars and other insect life
that these songbirds need to feed
their ravenous chicks. Even birds
that eat seeds and fruit the rest of
the year often switch to hunting
insects during breeding in order
to give their babies enough fat and
protein to thrive. Eastern deciduous forests are especially famous
for the wave of warblers that breed
there, and I have to say that I am

insanely jealous of this. In the West we have a dozen or so warbler species, but the East sees thirty or forty during the spring migration and breeding season. A greater diversity of tanagers, vireos, and orioles also can be found in eastern deciduous forests than out west. In the East, titmice often replace chickadees as the stars of mixed-species flocks—and they sound remarkably similar—so keep eyes and ears alert for them too.

## Riparian Areas

We already talked about wetlands, but riparian areas are a special kind of wetland that are usually considered separately from lakes, ponds, and marshes. Riparian specifically refers to streamside or riverside habitat that typically features moving water and, like other wetlands, can offer birders a huge bang for their birding buck because it provides an abundance of food, water, and shelter. Riparian zones usually host specific bird communities, but they often border the above-mentioned forests so that birds of several different habitats converge there.

Birding riparian areas *can* take special patience. Many birds like to stay hidden in the brush while others flit high above you and are difficult to see. Rivers and streams are very good places to observe and study various kinds of swallows and swifts, which hunt insects above and along rivers. Learning vocalizations can make a huge difference here—especially the songs of Yellow Warblers, Song Sparrows, Gray Catbirds, Willow Fly-catchers, vireos, waxwings, and blackbirds that frequent riparian areas. If you're next to a noisy stream or river—and if you are hearing compromised—you may not always hear the birds, but most species eventually show themselves.

### Grasslands

Grasslands, or prairies, are well-suited to "car birding," that is, driving around and viewing birds from the comfort of your vehicle—a terrific way to spot birds along rural roads and in other open spaces. Although in northern climes winter grasslands might net you a Snowy Owl, Rough-legged Hawks, or Snow Buntings, the best time to visit grasslands is spring and summer. Believe it or not, many shorebirds breed in grasslands this time of year. Here in Montana, we get to see breeding Long-billed Curlews, Willets, Marbled Godwits, and Upland Sandpipers to name a few. Sandhill Cranes inhabit grasslands in different parts of the country during different parts of the year as do Short-eared and Burrowing Owls. Grasslands, in general, are wonderful for viewing raptors, so keep an eye out for hawks, eagles, Northern Harriers, and a variety of falcons. If you're lucky, you'll flush grouse or pheasant from the side of the road.

Still, it's the LBBs—Little Brown Birds—that many of us associate with grasslands, and learning from more experienced birders can be especially useful in teasing out grassland species. Sparrows, pipits, meadowlarks, longspurs, Bobolinks, Dickcissels, Horned Larks, and Lark Buntings are favorite grassland birds. These birds prefer to stay down low much of the time, but one nice thing about most grasslands is that the roads through them are often conveniently lined with barbed-wire fences. Most LBBs—and a host of other birds—utilize these perches to sing for mates and defend territories.

When Braden and I see an LBB on the road or on a fence, we stop fifty or so yards away and try to identify it through our binoculars. Some species, such as Horned Larks, are relatively easy to pick out, but others can be tough (see Chapter 21: Tackling Difficult Birds, Group by Group). With practice, you'll begin to notice different kinds and qualities of grassland habitats and what kind of LBBs you can expect in each. Savannah Sparrows, for instance, prefer taller, slightly wetter grasslands while Vesper Sparrows inhabit shorter, drier conditions.

### Deserts

I almost didn't include deserts in this chapter because they vary so much, but Braden wouldn't hear of it, and the truth is that we've had wonderful desert birding experiences. Deserts come in an astonishing array of types, and each hosts its particular bird species. In Arizona's Sonoran Desert, with its forests of saguaros, you can find Gila Woodpeckers and

Gilded Flickers, along with an incredible variety of other birds including Curved-billed and Crissal Thrashers, Cactus Wrens, Black-throated Sparrows, Broad-billed Hummingbirds, Harris's Hawks, and Ferruginous Pygmy-Owls. Not to be outdone, the Mojave Desert, with its Joshua trees and miles of mesquite, boasts an equally rich avifauna: Sagebrush Sparrows,

LeConte's Thrashers, Black-tailed Gnatcatchers, Green-tailed Towhees, and Golden Eagles, to name a few. These two types of deserts share many species with each other and with the Great Basin Desert habitat that occupies much of the interior West from eastern California to Utah and up through Idaho. This magnificent, and underappreciated, desert is dominated by sagebrush and a plant called shadscale.

Because of the heat and dust, you might opt to mostly bird by car through the desert, but if the weather is nice, you'll learn a lot more by getting out for a walk. Just carry plenty of water, and wear protective boots in case you encounter a rattlesnake or two.

### Coastlines

Even though you will encounter many more different habitats than those listed above, I'm going to wrap up this brief survey with one of the most dynamic places to bird: coastlines.

Coastlines, of course, aren't just one thing. They consist of sandy beaches, rocky shores, saltwater marshes, mudflats, mangrove swamps, and other habitat types, but almost invariably they are places where you can find different birds from what you'll find inland. Gulls, for instance, can be found inland, but rarely in the variety that you find along the shore. The same can be said for plovers, sandpipers, terns, and other shorebirds.

Look out onto the water and you might see pelicans, cormorants, gannets, and with luck, pelagic species—those usually found far from shore. The alcid family—sometimes known as the "penguins of the north"—includes murres and murrelets, dovekies, guillemots, auklets, razorbills, and the most famous members of the group, puffins. These are most easily seen during an offshore cruise but can be spotted from shore in many places. Murrelets and auklets are West Coast only, but the other groups have representatives off both the Pacific and more northerly Atlantic states. If you find yourself on a rocky shore or a jetty, look for oystercatchers, Surfbirds, and Rock or Purple Sandpipers, depending on which coast you're on.

Spotting scopes come in especially handy on coastlines as you often have to scour a bird's finer details to identify it. Gulls are notorious for this since many are distinguished by eye color or subtle markings on their bills or feathers. We'll talk more about gulls and spotting scopes later!

One final, fascinating thing about coastlines is that winter is often the best time to bird there. During spring and summer, many birds are busy breeding in the Arctic or inland. Where do they spend the winters? You guessed it—coastlines. Scope the birds floating offshore and you might see some of the world's coolest ducks, including three kinds of scoters, two kinds of eiders (on the Atlantic), and Harlequin Ducks—spectacular creatures that in the Lower 48 breed only in a select few clean, whitewater streams. Loons are often much easier to find floating offshore in winter than they are on their interior breeding lakes and ponds.

## CHAPTER 14

# Bird-cations: America's Best Birding Destinations

As I've mentioned before, enjoying birds does not require huge outlays of cash, but if you have the means, birding provides plenty of opportunities to deplete your savings. My favorite? Visiting one of America's great birding destinations. Even if you cannot afford to do so now, you may want to consider saving up for such a trip.

One reason is that once you're bitten by the birding bug, you will start getting curious about distant birds even before you've mastered your local species. More critically, if you've reached my age, you understand that the next winter and spring could be your last, so you'd better damned well start planning your dream vacation while you're still breathing—a vacation that absolutely has to involve birding.

For me, birding and travel have become inseparable. The opportunity to see new birds gives me the added incentive I need to take off to a place I've never before explored. At the same time, birding gives me greater purpose and enjoyment when I travel to a place I was going to visit anyway.

Largely because of work-related opportunities, I have been fortunate to visit most, but not all, of the birding epicenters I share below. To make sure I didn't add too much of my own bias, I asked the Facebook Redpolling group for their favorites, and while the actual vote tallies surprised me,

the general consensus of "best places" did not. I'll give you a rundown of the entire list, but first let's focus on the top three.

## #1. Southeast Arizona/Southwest New Mexico
**Best Time to Visit: Late April through May**
I knew that southeast Arizona would rank highly on my poll, but I didn't know that it would obliterate the competition, garnering 27 percent of all votes. Then again, maybe that's not a surprise. In the swath of territory stretching roughly from Tucson south to Nogales and east to just over the New Mexico border, you can find a treasure trove of legendary birding sites. These include Ramsey Canyon, Madera Canyon, Patagonia Lake State Park, San Bernardino National Wildlife Refuge, the Chiricahua Mountains, and the tiny town of Portal—the hummingbird capital of the

US. This region's huge variety of desert and mountain habitats provides homes to a startling variety of birds and is the only part of the United States where you can reliably find Elegant Trogons, Mexican Chickadees, Olive Warblers, Whiskered Screech-Owls, Thick-billed Kingbirds, and many other species most commonly found in Mexico and parts south. The area also receives its share of rare vagrants—birds outside of their usual ranges—making it a place that competitive birders return to multiple times to rack up species. While some of the birding here can be quite rugged, the area also abounds with car-birding opportunities and centers that have set up bird feeders that lend themselves to people with mobil-

ity issues. Note that while Arizona's best birding happens in spring, the state boasts terrific birds all year round. If you are going to visit one part of the country specifically to bird, this is the one!

## #2. Rio Grande Valley, Texas
**Best Time to Visit: September through May**

The number-two choice for birders in my poll, garnering 20 percent of votes, also lies along the Mexican border. The Rio Grande Valley's decidedly tropical feel makes it irresistible to both birds and people needing a shot of sun. Even better, the vast majority of great birds here can be found from October through March, right when many of us face the choice of heading south or drinking ourselves to death.

Scads of bird migrants from the north winter in the Rio Grande Valley, as do year-round residents such as Green Jays, Audubon's and Altamira

Orioles, Great Kiskadees, Olive Sparrows, and White-tailed Hawks. If you don't visit in April or May, you'll miss many migrating songbirds, but don't sweat it. You'll probably catch some of them back home anyway. Must-see hotspots include, but are not limited to, South Padre Island, Laguna Atascosa National Wildlife Refuge, Resaca de la Palma State Park, Santa Ana National Wildlife Refuge, Estero Llano Grande State Park, and the private

Salineño Wildlife Preserve. To help you plan your trip, Texas Parks and Wildlife has created an outstanding series of "birding trail" maps for different parts of the state (see Bird-Related Websites in Resources).

## #3. Houston/High Island/Bolivar Peninsula, Texas

**Best Time to Visit: Late April/Early May (but most times of year except June and July can be very good, especially for shorebirds and seabirds)**
Remarkably, no other choice on my poll hit double digit tallies, but the greater Houston megalopolis probably should have. Braden and I have a special fondness for Houston, not only because of its amazing Tex-Mex food and barbecue, but because it was the first place we traveled specifically to watch spring migration. The entire Houston area is loaded with great birding spots, but during migration most people head to High Island. Houston Audubon (houstonaudubon.org) manages reserves here that have become the focus for a kind of month-long birding frenzy that attracts upwards of ten thousand birders per

year from all over the country and the world.

High Island itself is a key resting and refueling stop for migrating songbirds completing their epic journeys across the Gulf of Mexico, but part of what makes the area so special is that dozens of seabirds, shorebirds, and waders can be found just down the road at the tip of the Bolivar Peninsula. Oh, and did I mention that Anahuac and several other national wildlife refuges sit right next door?

I recommend staying in the tiny town of Winnie, which hosts several solid hotels and a donut shop. For added fun, take the ferry from Port Bolivar to Galveston Island, with its own wealth of great birding hotspots.

Back on High Island, Houston Audubon has provided an incredible wheelchair-friendly canopy walkway that gives bird's-eye views of songbirds that like to hang out in the treetops and of the extensive rookery where Roseate Spoonbills, Tricolored Herons, Snowy Egrets, and other wading birds nest each year.

Beyond these top-three choices, it's an impossible task to round up all of the country's great birding destinations in one short chapter, but perhaps the best attempt can be made thematically.

## Other Great Migration Destinations

The entire Gulf Coast teems with migrating songbirds in spring and to a lesser extent in the fall. Popular locations most frequently mentioned in my poll include Dauphin Island (Alabama), Cameron Parish (Louisiana), and St. Marks National Wildlife Refuge (Florida).

Not all great migration spots are located on the Gulf Coast, however. Cape May, New Jersey, is world famous for large numbers of migrating songbirds and shorebirds in both spring and fall. Thanks to the Black Swamp Bird Observatory, northwest Ohio also attracts plenty of migration seekers. Its Biggest Week in American Birding festival, I'm told, is an experience not to be missed.

One of the most fun things Braden and I have ever done is bird New York City in early May. We hit migration just right and scored dozens of songbird species, including several new warblers for my life list. Most of these birds were in Central Park and Brooklyn's Prospect Park, but we ran into migrants in "postage-stamp parks," on the High Line elevated trail, along the waterfront, and almost everywhere else we looked.

## Other Great Winter Destinations

I've already mentioned south Texas as a great winter birding location, but the entire West Coast mounts stiff competition. Braden and I have had impressive trips to San Diego, Santa Barbara, the Bay Area, and coastal Oregon in winter and always found tons of permanent and overwintering species. Meanwhile, California's Central Valley refuges fill up with waterfowl and shorebirds in fall and winter. If you're near San Jose, be sure to chase down California Condors, Yellow-billed Magpies, and Lawrence's Goldfinches. I haven't personally birded South Florida in winter, but species checklists reveal that it hosts hundreds of species. In contrast, if you're after Great Gray Owls and other winter specialties, you might try Minnesota's Sax-Zim Bog—or head to my home state of Montana.

## Hawai'i

As you can imagine, our fiftieth state is a wonderful year-round birding destination but was added to the official ABA Area only in 2017—and not without controversy. While Hawai'i evolved dozens of fabulous endemic bird species, including its world-famous honeycreepers, many are either extinct or so rare that you and I will probably never see them in the wild. The majority of birds you will add to your life list in Hawai'i are exotic

# Alaska

Alaska. Whew. Where to begin? With currently a mind-blowing 567 species reported, Alaska truly is its own nation when it comes to birding. Both because of its northern location and its proximity to Asia, it is home to dozens of species that you won't find anywhere else in America. Sarah Palin didn't really see Russia from her home in Alaska—but she might have seen some Russian birds!

Many Alaska birding locations and trips are fairly accessible. "The best single wildlife-watching day of my life was taking a boat tour on Resurrection Bay out of Seward," opines biologist Harley Winfrey, who spent a summer working in Alaska's Interior. Alaska resident and environmental consultant Andy Bankert adds, "On the road system, you can see some great stuff like all three ptarmigans, wheatears, and Surfbirds in the mountains above Anchorage. Other than close to Anchorage, there is abundant free roadside camping, although rental cars might be expensive."

Despite this birding abundance, Alaska may be a place where you want to make use of a birding tour or guide, as many locations are remote and challenging to negotiate. "It really depends on how much money you have to spend," says Bankert. "The road system is great, but flying away from the main roads is even better. If you can afford to travel away from the roads, Nome and [the island of] St. Paul are my two favorite places. St. Paul has great looks at alcids and kittiwakes and is pretty much set up through the local tour company, but in Nome you can just rent a car and camp almost anywhere outside of town."

Although I haven't yet mustered the courage or financial resources to tackle Alaska myself, I gather that it's best to plan separate trips to Nome, the Southeast, Utqiagvik (Barrow), the Interior, and the Aleutians. "Don't try to do it all at once!" cautions my Facebook pal Christian Roberts, an avid birder from Dallas. "Trying to cram in the Kenai Peninsula, Adak, and Nome will be too much on one trip, but if you could do something like Denali and the Anchorage/Seward area in a week, you could see a ton of crazy stuff."

If you want to get started searching for a guide, one that comes highly recommended is Aaron Lang of Wilderness Birding Adventures (wildernessbirding.com). For more information on where to start, you might also consult a book such as George C. West's *A Birder's Guide to Alaska* (if you can find a copy) or Lynn E. Barber's newer *Big Years, Biggest States: Birding in Texas and Alaska*.

imports such as the Warbling White-eye, Saffron Finch, and Yellow-fronted Canary. Still, you can pick up a few cool Hawaiian natives such as the Hawaiian Coot and Nene (Hawaiian Goose), as well as birds that are challenging to find elsewhere in the US such as the Pacific Golden-Plover (in winter), Laysan Albatross, and Red-footed Booby.

## Birding Festivals

Although you can easily arrange to visit most US birding destinations yourself, sometimes it's nice to have a birding itinerary all laid out for you. Enter the birding festival. Birding festivals cater to all types of birders, but are especially suited to newer birders and those of us creeping up there in years. That's because festival organizers usually figure out places for you to stay and offer a nice variety of birding experiences to choose from, including lectures, workshops, birding trips—even wine-and-cheese parties. All you have to do is get there and hand over your credit card.

Flipping through my most recent issues of *Birding* and *Bird Watcher's Digest* (BWD), I encountered ads for a dozen different festivals all over the country—but there are far more than that. Braden and I have participated in several and have even acted as field trip leaders. Our verdict: These festivals are a lot of fun. At most of them, registering for the festival allows you to attend keynotes and other lectures at no extra cost, and the festival's

HQ is often in a hotel that offers discounted rooms for participants. Vendors set up in a central area much as they would at any other conference.

It's the extra outings, however, that are a festival's main events. These can vary from pelagic cruises—if, say, you are at the San Diego or Monterey Bay festivals—to excursions to local wildlife refuges and other hotspots. Some outings target hard-to-find birds while others are aimed at birders who want to check off as many species as possible for their life lists. On one all-day tour that Braden and I helped guide at the San Diego Bird Festival, our group tallied more than 130 species in a single day! On another trip at the Monterey Bay Birding Festival, we cracked 90 species. For these outings, birders either caravan in their own cars, or more often, pile into a bus that transports them to their destination.

Bird festivals vary greatly in intensity. High Island in spring kind of functions as a month-long high-octane festival where most people are focused on finding every bird possible. You just show up, buy a patch to give you entry into the locations run by Houston Audubon, and bird till you drop. I imagine Ohio's Biggest Week in Birding is similarly intense, as is the Rio Grande Valley Birding Festival in Harlingen, Texas, which over the course of five days boasts 120 field trips—gasp!

In contrast, I recently participated in the HummerBird Celebration in Rockport, Texas, and found it delightfully relaxed. Organizers provided maps for visitors to self-tour various yards with great hummingbird feeder setups. They also offered a variety of outings for people who liked birds, but weren't necessarily hard-core birders. I co-led one of these trips out to a nearby ranch, where we boarded open trailers pulled by tractors, and everyone had a lovely time. Braden and I have had similar experiences at the annual Wings Across the Big Sky festival put on by Montana Audubon.

Give a festival a try. You'll see a lot of cool birds, explore new parts of the country, and no doubt meet some like-minded fellow birders. Just writing this makes me look forward to my next birding festival experience!

## CHAPTER 15

# Bird Tours, Guides, Lodges, and Cruises

Going on a professionally run bird tour is the next step up from attending a festival and will likely make a bigger dent in your credit limit. Cost, in fact, has prevented me from embarking on such a tour, as even the cheapest cost thousands, or even tens of thousands, of dollars. The other thing about some bird tours is they can be exhausting dawn-to-dusk affairs, and as a Boomer who cherishes my afternoon naps, I rarely want to be birding that intensely day after day.

That doesn't mean I wouldn't love to go on a birding tour sometime, especially to a country I've never visited—and on a tour that caters to "nap-oriented" birders such as myself. The ABA offers a range of domestic and international tours and ranks the pace of each as low, medium, or high. Another well-regarded outfit, Tropical Birding Tours, also runs a large variety of tours rated at different intensities, but customized tours are a big part of their business. So if you've got the bucks, they'll probably do whatever you wish.

A host of independent operators also will arrange any kind of trip that you want. If you're considering a tour out of the country, be sure to ask how they operate in ways that benefit local guides and communities. In the past, some "ecotour" outfits have built up nasty reputations by swooping in to lead a bunch of *yanquis* on a rainforest adventure or something while cutting out local guides, who often know far more about the local fauna. Today, there's greater awareness of this kind of economic imperialism, but do your due diligence before making your reservations.

## Booking Local Guides

Here's a little-known secret: you do not need to go on a birding tour to arrange the services of a guide. On both of my family's trips to South America, I booked local guides to show us the best of the birds. At the end of our Galápagos cruise, for example, we had a layover afternoon in Guayaquil, Ecuador, and I arranged with bird guide Paul Abad to pick me and Braden up at our hotel. Abad proved to be an absolute delight and drove us in his comfortable 4WD vehicle to Cerro Blanco National Park outside the city. Gray conditions made birding tough, but thanks to Abad we managed to see twenty-nine species, most of them lifers. We had so much fun that when we returned to South America the following year, we

hired different guides in Cuzco, Peru, and Mindo, Ecuador, and had terrific experiences with each.

Hiring guides has several distinct benefits. First, it allows you to have top-quality birding experiences even in the midst of what might be a "nonbirding" vacation. Second, it lets you meet authentic, local people. Third, they often know hotspots that outside operators do not. Last, it can save you serious money over a full-on birding tour, and you can take satisfaction that the money is going directly into the pockets of people who actually live and work there. How good is that?

You may be asking, "But how do I find a reputable bird guide?" Often your hotel can arrange one for you, but I've usually used the internet. Almost any "birdy" area will have a local guide or service listed online. When you find one, check out the reviews to get a feel for if the person or company is legit. You can also ask around for recommendations, either through your personal connections or on social media forums focused on birding.

Travel, of course, always carries some risk, but I have found that most fears of traveling in foreign countries are overblown. On the other hand, the rewards of venturing out like this, provided you do your research and use common sense, almost always lead to amazing experiences you will never forget.

## Lodges, Cruises, and Other Expeditions

Before closing this chapter, I should mention two more ways to see birds, especially in foreign countries. A happy medium between going on a birding tour and hiring an occasional local bird guide is staying at an ecolodge. Lodges, like tours, can be expensive, but they offer activities for all members of the family. Again, I urge you to find lodges owned and operated by residents of the area you're visiting. When we went to the Amazon region of Ecuador, we stayed at the Sani Lodge, owned and operated by the eponymous Indigenous community. It wasn't quite as fancy as the five-star place upriver, but Sani handled the travel arrangements extremely well, and the guides and food were excellent. Even better, I knew that the money went to supporting the local community and its conservation efforts.

Ecocruises are essentially lodges that float, and are usually more expensive. The only one we've been on was courtesy of my in-laws to the aforementioned Galápagos. I've got to say it was one of the highlights of my life. The trip didn't focus on birds, but a lot of the action centered on them, and we had memorable experiences with frigatebirds, Galápagos Penguins, various Galápagos finches, Brown Noddies, and three kinds of boobies. Our cruise was run by Lindblad Expeditions, a partner of National Geographic, and I only mention them here in the hopes that they will send me on another wonderful nature cruise free of charge. (Hint: South Georgia Island.)

Other experienced companies offer both land and sea expeditions under a model of sustainable tourism. Many itineraries aren't specifically aimed at birds—but you will nonetheless see plenty to fill out your life list! If you're looking for and can afford such an experience, check them out.

# PART V

# BIRDING AROUND BARRIERS

*Society as a whole benefits immeasurably from a climate in which all persons, regardless of race, gender, or physical ability may have the opportunity to earn respect, responsibility, exercise, and enjoyment based on birding.*
—*Sandra Day O'Connor*

## CHAPTER 16

# Birding for All

I wrote this book to be a complete guide for *all* beginning birders, especially those in the second half of life. But it wouldn't truly be complete if we didn't acknowledge some of the unique barriers that affect our abilities to bird, regardless of age, and share some ideas for overcoming them. A wonderful companion resource for this section is the Birdability website (birdability.org), which goes to great lengths to provide helpful information and encouragement to birders of all abilities and backgrounds. I encourage you to check it out.

Perhaps none of these topics is as urgent as inclusivity. Social, economic, racial, and sexual orientation barriers prevent people of all ages from taking up and enjoying a variety of outdoor activities, including birding. No matter our ethnicity, orientation, or economic situations, we cannot afford to let that keep happening.

## Birding While Black

The highly publicized 2020 incident in New York City's Central Park between Christian Cooper, who is Black and gay, and Amy Cooper (no relation), who is white and straight, provided a much-needed wake-up call for me and many others in the birding community. While out birding in a section of the park known as the Ramble, Christian politely asked Amy to leash her dog in accordance with park rules. She refused and then, as he began to film her, called the police to complain that an African American man was threatening her and her dog. It was a crass display and, the public learned, the tip of the iceberg in what nonwhite birders face in this country.

The incident helped inspire a group of Black birders and STEM professionals to create the first Black Birders Week, a series of events designed to counter the idea that "Black people don't belong" in the outdoors, to educate other birders and the broader community about challenges Black birders face, and to increase diversity in birding and conservation. I gotta say, watching the panel recordings from this inaugural event opened my eyes as a white birder. I had no idea to what lengths many people of color must go simply to enjoy the outdoors safely.

The panelists, both students and professors, related multiple incidents in which they had been verbally assaulted and targeted by police because they were "birding while Black." In order to avoid suspicion, most said that they took great care to "look like a birder" before going out, and even then they received excessive scrutiny. At least one person flat-out said that he would not bird in certain states for fear of his safety.

J. Drew Lanham is a distinguished professor of wildlife ecology and master teacher in the Forestry and Environmental Conservation Department at Clemson University and the recipient of a prestigious MacArthur Foundation Fellowship. He also is an avid Boomer ornithologist, poet, and the author of *The Home Place: Memoirs of a Colored Man's Love Affair with Nature*. However, it was his short 2013 *Orion* magazine article "9 Rules for the Black Birdwatcher" that especially attracted the attention of the wider birding community.

In the piece, he succinctly offers advice about how to bird safely and gives wry insights into what people of color face when they go out birding, like sometimes being confused for "the other Black birder." Regarding safety, he recommends always wearing binoculars, carrying three forms of identification, and never wearing a hoodie. He also issues a strict "no-no" about birding after dark. Wearing binoculars and carrying ID are good advice for *any* birder, especially if exploring new territory—but as Lanham points out, if such gear is not present, it does not usually carry the potentially deadly consequences as it does for people of color. Listen to the American Birding Podcast episode with Lanham, titled "Birding While Black with J. Drew Lanham" (see Resources).

In a conversation I had with Helen Drummond, the director of the Houston Audubon Society and one of the most visible Black women working in conservation, she suggested, "I would encourage people to bird with a group, especially as one is getting to know a new area. Also get to know your local Audubon chapter. If you're just beginning, get started in your own community and neighborhood, places where you are already comfortable. What's great about birds is that they are everywhere."

## LGBTQ+ Birding

Like BIPOC members of our society, LGBTQ+ people have faced extreme prejudice and discrimination. As birders, however, their challenges have been a bit different. Malcolm Hodges formed the group, Gaggle, in Atlanta in 1995 to fulfill a dream of starting an LGBTQ+ birding club, and because he thought it would be fun to go birding with other "out-queer folks."

"I think the challenges faced by BIPOC birders are not entirely comparable to those of queer birders, and in some ways more difficult to overcome," he explained to me. "Queer birders often 'pass' in regular bird clubs and communities because birders talk mostly about birds and avoid personal topics."

This has not prevented them from feeling isolated and alone, however, and sometimes afraid to come out to others in their birding communities. Groups such as the Gaggle and a spin-off, Queer Birders of North America, have sought to overcome this problem. "We [the Gaggle] provide a safe space to be out and queer while birding," Hodges says, "and that seems to be something enjoyed by queer birders, in Atlanta at least." The group has about 140 members and is loosely organized, getting together for potlucks a couple times a year to plan local and regional outings for the following six months.

As far as safety in the US, Hodges says that the Gaggle community exercises the same precautions that any LGBTQ+ people would take in outdoors and rural situations—but adds that he doesn't know of any who have been abused or assaulted so far. The situation can be a lot scarier abroad, as more than sixty countries have laws that criminalize homosexuality. These include quite a few places that are great birding destinations and are therefore potentially off-limits to LGBTQ+ birders.

And even though acceptance of the LGBTQ+ community has improved here at home and in many other countries, there is still work to be done. Hodges encourages other LGBTQ+ birders to start their own groups, and says that the Gaggle is happy to offer advice and support.

"Creating opportunities for nonwhite [and/or non-]straight birders to go out in a supportive group can allow them to go to places where they would feel uncomfortable alone. Just by existing, the Gaggle allows birders to see that queers are part of the greater birding community and opens the door for young people to get outdoors and outside themselves, especially during the difficult years of queer adolescence."

Speaking of young people, widespread recent attacks on trans and nonbinary youth pose a particularly tough challenge. Hodges encourages young queer birders to seek out other groups of young birders, such as at birding camps, adding, "Young people are generally more supportive of their LGBTQ+ peers than are some older birders, and [young queer birders] may find it easier to be out in such settings."

Meanwhile, straight birders can offer support on important social issues that impact LGBTQ+ birders, in part by promoting inclusivity and a welcoming atmosphere in our own birding communities. We also can learn a thing or two from the Gaggle. "We have gradually had more straight birders joining us," Hodges says, "likely because they enjoy the more cooperative, noncompetitive way we bird and how much fun we have. I guess about a quarter of those on our field trips are not queer, just friends and allies."

Both the Gaggle and Queer Birders of North America can be contacted through their Facebook pages. For an excellent discussion on queer birding, listen to the American Birding Podcast episode "Affinity and Identity in the QBNA with Jennifer Rycenga and Michael Retter" (see Resources).

## Birding Around Economic and Financial Barriers

Barriers to birding extend beyond racism and gender discrimination. People in many underserved—more properly called disinvested—communities often don't have access to nature or suffer from inadequate education about the natural world. This situation can arise from many factors including geographic isolation, economic stagnation, and underfunding for education, parks, and other services. It can affect people of all races and backgrounds and is particularly difficult to change.

Often, an interest in birding is sparked by some kind of personal connection or interaction. Houston Audubon's Helen Drummond explained the importance of reaching people who may not have a connection to nature, which can be a sensitive topic. "The key to interacting with communities is building relationships. And part of building relationships is listening. It's understanding what [the community's] interests are, what their everyday concerns are, and identifying that common link that can connect our interests to their concerns. That's number one. And you have to be genuine about it. I know oftentimes we'll go into a community or anywhere with *our* vision and *our* mission in mind, right? And we want to 'bring them along.' That's how we think. So we need to look at communities more comprehensively and realize that human beings are complex. We're multifaceted. So are communities."

Houston Audubon is a great example of how creating birding relationships can happen. Their initiatives range from visiting schools and organizing field trips to setting up a raptor center in a disinvested part of the city. These projects are designed to help people of all backgrounds learn about birds and connect with nature. They provide a great model for what groups and individuals can do to improve the world for both birds and people.

## Welcoming Everyone to the Flock

Birding is an activity that everyone can and should enjoy. Beyond the obvious social-justice implications, protecting and saving birds will take efforts from all of us—no matter who you are or where you come from. Groups such as the Audubon Society and the ABA have taken real steps to increase outreach and representation in their organizations, but what can *you* do to make a difference?

One place to begin is to recognize that *all* birders need to have a no-tolerance attitude to any form of discrimination when out birding and cultivate an environment where all feel welcome. How that manifests for each of us will be different depending on experience, means, community, and other

factors. For some, our biggest influence may come from face-to-face interactions with others. As I describe in more detail in Chapter 31: Leading Bird Trips and Teaching Classes, I've been fortunate to have opportunities to teach other people about birds and birding in several capacities. Many of my students have been young people from a variety of backgrounds, and when I am out birding or leading a birding trip, I do my best to treat everyone as a fellow birder without making assumptions about their background or expertise.

These kinds of experiences make me optimistic that the dial is moving and that birding is becoming both safer and more inclusive. We can't take our foot off the gas, however. If you're reading this, I encourage you to think about your own circumstances, expertise, and connections and what makes sense for you to do. One huge advantage to birding is that it is very inexpensive to pursue, requiring at its most basic a pair of binoculars. The simple act of donating some optics to a birding club or to a kid who shows an interest in birding could make a positive difference in a person's life. Joining groups such as your local Audubon Society chapter or volunteering your birding skills at a community or senior citizen center can help you get even more involved.

## CHAPTER 17

# Physical Limitations I: Dealing with Hearing Loss

While racial, gender, and economic inequities impact specific groups of people, physical impairments eventually affect us all, and one of the most widespread issues older and many not-so-older birders face is hearing loss. Although the purpose of this book is to provide a complete guide for the beginning birder, if I could single out one issue that compelled me to write it, it would be my own struggles with hearing loss. As I recounted, my hearing loss likely occurred from firing guns without ear protection, but it doesn't really matter what causes such a loss. Once our hearing has been damaged, that loss is permanent. Our bodies cannot heal or regrow the sensory hairs or any other elements of our auditory systems.

Losing the upper range of my hearing was much more than an inconvenience. It took a serious emotional toll on me. I'd just discovered this passion that I planned to pursue the rest of my life, and suddenly fate deprived me of a huge part of that enjoyment and intellectual activity— and I had to acknowledge that it was never coming back.

Losing the ability to do something *forever*, in fact, seriously made me confront mortality, perhaps for the first time. And while in the big picture, this preview to death might make me appreciate life more and be an important part of my personal development, in the short term it was frustrating, depressing, and terrifying.

Fortunately, after tearing out what was left of my hair and swearing at the universe, I learned to *mostly* come to terms with my new situation. My hearing limitations still bother me, but not like they did for the first couple of years. And they inspired me to consider birding through the lens of limitations of all kinds, and realize that many "birding disabilities" can be accommodated through technology and a bit of strategizing.

In fact, I will make a bold statement here and say that today, *birding is within the grasp of anyone who wants to do it, no matter what your disadvantages or differing abilities might be*

A conversation I had with digital audio engineer Harold Mills helped add perspective to the sensory limitations I and other humans face. Mills, a graduate of Cornell University, has worked extensively at creating software and hardware to detect and identify bird vocalizations, and has recently begun to lose some of his own high-frequency hearing.

"It's driven home the fact that even the person with the best hearing is very limited," he told me. "They can't hear bats, and they can't hear very high-frequency insects. And the person with the best vision can't see things in the ultraviolet. There's a lot happening outside the range of *normal* human perception, much less *limited* human perception. In a sense what you can perceive is all relative."

I remind myself of this every time I miss a bird's call or fail to spot one in a green leafy tree, and you know what? It helps me feel better.

If you're in a similar boat, here are some tips for getting through.

## The Miracle of Hearing Aids

The most common form of hearing loss, called sensorineural hearing loss, results from damage to the sensory hairs of the inner ear or the nerves that connect them to the brain. It's the kind of hearing loss that I and tens of millions of other people experience, and usually results from extreme or prolonged exposure to loud noise or age-related deterioration of our auditory systems.

Cochlear implants and other surgical procedures are reserved for those with profound deafness and will not help the typical birder, but most hearing loss can be mitigated with hearing aids. Modern hearing aids are basically little amplifiers that magnify the sounds reaching your ears. Like a lot of people these days, I bought my hearing aids at Costco and have been quite happy with them. Not only can my audiologist adjust the amplification for the degree of hearing loss I have at each frequency, but he programmed settings for different situations—including birding.

At least three factors do still limit the utility of hearing aids:

- They cannot make up for a complete loss of the ear's sensory hairs at a particular frequency, no matter how much you crank up the volume.
- Because they pick up sounds via tiny microphones pointed in fixed directions, they often make the location of bird vocalizations difficult to pinpoint.
- Bird songs are often so complex that even with hearing aids, you may not hear the complete song that healthy ears can.

This last point is especially worth expanding on. I never have heard, and probably never will hear, a Golden-crowned Kinglet or Brown Creeper in the wild. I also cannot hear the complete songs of many other birds unless I am very close, even with my hearing aids in. Because of this, what I learn as the song of, say, a Hermit Thrush, may be quite different from what a person with healthy ears experiences.

My hearing also continues to change year to year, so I have to reanalyze and relearn certain bird vocalizations that sound different from one month or year to the next. Needless to say, this is frustrating—but still a lot better than hearing nothing at all.

Cost can be a significant factor in a person's decision to buy hearing aids, but even as I write this, hearing aid technology is rapidly evolving and becoming much more affordable. Over-the-counter hearing aids are now available online, at drugstores, and through other retail outlets. Many designs connect to other devices using Bluetooth, allowing the aids to double as headphones, earbuds, and other technology. Some online companies also provide less expensive hearing aids that can be programmed via online hearing tests, meaning you never have to see a hearing professional.

Comparing and contrasting all of these options is way beyond the scope of this book and would be out of date by the time you read it. I will say that when it comes to hearing aids, you probably get what you pay for, and I still recommend seeing a hearing specialist if you can afford it and/or your insurance covers it.

You should also check out current reviews of hearing aids that are available through the National Council on Aging (ncoa.org) and other organizations.

My main point is this: If it seems like everyone around you is mumbling, *do not wait* to get your ears checked and, if appropriate, buy some hearing aids. On average, a person with hearing loss waits *ten years* before they seek the help of a hearing professional. Cost, stigma, and the fact that health insurance often doesn't cover hearing aids all play into this situation. But once your brain stops hearing a certain frequency, it begins cutting the neural connections for processing that frequency. Once those connections are gone, they most likely will never grow back, so take action!

## Hearing Help Apps

Hearing aids are not the only valuable tool for a birder with hearing loss. Sound ID, part of the Merlin app we discussed earlier, can be a profound help to someone with hearing loss because of how it can identify birds in real time without connection to a cell tower. Even with my phone's relatively weak microphone, the app detects bird vocalizations that I cannot

# Hear Birds Again

In the early 1990s well-known nature recordist Lang Elliott worked with partner Hugh Sussman to develop a machine called the SongFinder. The SongFinder took high-frequency sounds and translated them into lower frequencies that more birders can hear, and the device earned a small but loyal following for almost thirty years. Elliott and Sussman finally decided to put the SongFinder out of production, but Elliott, who has high-frequency hearing loss, teamed up with signal processing engineer Harold Mills to come up with a new invention: a phone-based app called Hear Birds Again.

Like its predecessor, Hear Birds Again takes high frequencies and transcribes them into lower frequencies. As I write this, the app has been released for iPhone, with plans for an Android version as time and resources allow. For the best results, the developers highly recommend using what they call a "bineural headset," which offers high-fidelity sound in a way that you can pinpoint a bird's location in a three-dimensional space. I have not yet experimented with this, but for more information, check out the website hearbirdsagain.org.

hear, alerting me to which birds to look for around me. When I do hear a call but am unsure what it is, the app can help confirm my ID or indicate that I may be on the wrong track.

By having a quick, albeit provisional, confirmation, I can continually retrain my brain on what I am hearing, even as the sounds of vocalizations seem to change for me over time. Every spring, for instance, I have to relearn how to distinguish the sharp calls of Evening Grosbeaks from those of Northern Flickers. If I suspect a grosbeak, I punch up Sound ID and get a quick, fist-pumping "Yeah!"

Even though Sound ID seems to be accurate about 90 percent of the time, I never use it as the sole basis for an identification—and you shouldn't either. I don't add a bird to my checklist until I see it for myself or get close enough to identify a song I am sure that I know. Still, the app is a wonderful detection and confirmation aid that only recently became available, and hearing-impaired birders should take full advantage of it.

If Sound ID interests you, also take a look at BirdNET (https://bird net.cornell.edu/), a similar citizen-science, AI, birdsong-detection tool developed by other researchers at Cornell Lab and Chemnitz University in Germany.

## CHAPTER 18

# Physical Limitations II: Eyesight Issues

According to information posted on the Centers for Disease Control website, ninety million Americans over the age of forty have vision and eye problems—that's three in five people. More than four million suffer from eye and vision issues that cannot be corrected, but an astounding *eight million* have unresolved issues such as near- or far-sightedness, astigmatism, and presbyopia that could be easily corrected with eyeglasses, contact lenses, or surgery. So, in case you missed my similar message in the last chapter, the first thing I want to say to Boomers, geezers, and others reading this is *Go get your frickin' vision checked!*

Personally, I have been fortunate in the vision department. Like most people my age, I have presbyopia—age-related far-sightedness—so I have to carry around a pair of reading glasses for close-in viewing, but my mid- and far-range vision remain solid, a distinct advantage for a birder. Nonetheless, many of my fellow birders have vision issues that require added finagling. This is especially true for birders who wear glasses.

Some birders with glasses are able to quickly whip them off, holding them in one hand while using the binoculars like a pair of "super glasses." Others, such as Montana birder and former birding instructor Kristi DuBois, employ a different strategy. "I leave my glasses on," she explains, "as I have too much astigmatism to go without them, and am too near-sighted to spot the birds and get the binocs pointed in the right direction." For DuBois, having binoculars with long eye relief is especially important. Eye relief refers to the little tubes, or eyecups, that can be pulled or twisted out or in on binoculars, and are incredibly useful in fixing the right distance between one's eyeglasses and the binocular eyepieces.

For others, eye issues are a bit more complicated. My occasional birding buddy Steve Flood is one of those smart guys who started birding when he was young, but throughout his birding career he has had to juggle a whole basket of vision-related issues. He is near-sighted, with a –10 prescription. He suffered a detached retina that required laser surgery in 1983. He also sees a lot of "floaters" that make it difficult to see small or distant birds against gray or light skies. Oh yeah, and like many of us, he also requires reading glasses. How does he deal with all of these issues?

"I wear both glasses and contacts, and the daily choice is dictated by what activities I plan to be engaged in," Flood explains. "If I have to constantly switch back and forth from distant vision to near [reading] vision I will often choose my progressive-lens glasses because if I wore contacts on such a day, I would have to have +1 readers at the constant ready, which is cumbersome and slow." He switches up this strategy on days when it is raining or he is going back and forth from the cold outside air to a warm car. Then he chooses contacts to avoid the problem of his glasses fogging up and need-

# Totally Blind Birding

I recently came across an article on the Audubon website about an incredible series of trails in Colombia that cater to blind birders. Juan Pablo Culasso, a nature recordist from Uruguay, is almost totally blind and is unable to distinguish the shapes or colors of birds. He teamed up with several Colombian partners to create obstacle-free trails with rope guides to allow blind birders total independence as they move from birding spot to birding spot. The team also created an audio guide with the vocalizations of fifty common bird species found in the region.

This example not only serves as inspiration for other communities around the globe to create similarly accessible sites, it reinforces how "reachable" birding is for many of those with severe visual impairment.

If you are blind but have healthy hearing, learning to bird by ear is not only eminently doable, in some ways it provides a distinct advantage to those of us who depend mainly on sight to identify species. Not only are many trails, especially in urban areas, accessible for easy walking, but birders generally hear birds more often than we see them, especially in heavily forested areas. Culasso can identify more than seven hundred bird species by sound—a level of expertise I can only dream about!

Birding can bring huge emotional and psychological benefits to those who are blind or have low vision. In another Audubon article, legally blind birder Trevor Attenberg describes his own journey into birding and how it helped him feel much more connected to the world. In Trevor's case, it even led him to a career studying how birds help connect humans to nature.

ing frequent wiping. He emphasizes that neither of these choices interferes with his use of binoculars or a scope, as he can easily wear glasses or contacts with each.

My college roommate Roger Kohn succumbed to my birding evangelism several years ago, even though he has astigmatism in both eyes, which means his vision is blurry at all distances. When I asked him how he compensated for this, he replied, "I haven't needed a strategy per se other than making sure I bought binoculars that have eye relief." Birding without glasses isn't an option for him, but the eye relief tubes make it "a breeze."

He reassures other birders, "Wearing corrective lenses will not affect your birding enjoyment and learning in any way. As long as your impairment can be corrected with glasses, you're good to go. I just wish it wasn't so hard to keep the damn things clean!"

## CHAPTER 19

# Physical Limitations III: The Broken-Down Bod

When considering the physical birding challenges for those of us "of a certain age," we have to look beyond sensory system failures such as hearing and eyesight and consider injuries, other medical conditions, and just plain old wear and tear on our bodies.

I loved my forties. They were probably my best decade—except for the fact that I hadn't yet discovered birding! The one thing I did *not* like is that about one new thing started going wrong with my body every year. Granted, most of my issues were minor and could be accommodated fairly easily: acid reflux, a wonky shoulder, and my personal favorite, hemorrhoids!

By the time we're in our fifties and sixties, however, chances are that something more serious has cropped up, such as bad knees, hip replacements, diseases, and heart conditions. Perhaps you had a fall or were in an accident or, as in my case, permanently messed up your back while shoveling snow. Maybe you've been stricken by chronic fatigue syndrome, cancer, long COVID, or some other debilitating condition. Many of our military veterans face severe, permanent disabilities that most of us can't even comprehend.

What does this mean for your future as a birder?

Well, on one hand, it can make birding more difficult. If you are a wheelchair user or have extremely low energy, you may not be able to hike up to a mountain pass to see Boreal Chickadees and White-tailed Ptarmigans. If you have severe pain from arthritis or an old wound, you may not feel comfortable walking on a gravel path or uneven ground.

On the other hand, there's a high likelihood that birding will make your body healthier, no matter what physical condition you are in. One of my favorite quotes from 1960s health icon Jack LaLanne is, "The only way you can hurt your body is if you don't use it."

Okay, maybe LaLanne was drinking a bit too much of his own Kool-Aid, but the older I get, the more I appreciate his insights. In my early fifties, for example, I started experiencing regular knee pain, and I thought, "Well, shit, I'm going to need knee replacements by the time I hit sixty or sixty-five." Then I started birding and began hiking five or ten miles a week in pursuit of my avian quarry. Guess what? My knee pain disappeared. Turns out that my knees weren't wearing out. Instead, the stabilizing muscles around them had begun to atrophy from disuse! Birding, however, strengthened my legs and reduced the wear and tear on my knees, keeping the pain away.

I'm no doctor, and you should consult with your own physician about whatever ails you, but according to most general wellness experts, the more you walk, hike, and move around, the healthier you will be. It's no surprise that birding is great for that. Although you *can* bird by sitting in one place, most birders eventually want to find birds through exploration, whether that's walking through a park, hiking up a mountainside, bicycling along a river, or propelling a wheelchair on a boardwalk. This exercise makes almost every part of your body stronger, from your joints to your heart. It also is one of the best things I have found for improving my mental health. What's not to love?

## Easing into Activity

With the pep-talk part of this chapter out of the way, let's get to a few common-sense tips for dealing with physical challenges:

- If you are not used to doing much walking or hiking, start gradually. Before I plan to hike up a mountain, I do smaller training hikes up hills for a week or three to avoid injury and distress on the day of the climb. If you are really out of shape, start with short walks on flat ground before heading out for longer walks. *And again, if you have any kind of medical issues, consult with your doctor before doing anything beyond your ordinary routine.*
- Bring walking sticks or trekking/hiking poles to help you with steep or uneven terrain. Even if your joints and muscles are healthy, "sticks" lessen the pressure on your legs while giving your arms a bit of a workout. They can also help with balance issues and prevent falls, especially while going downhill. I now use them with almost any walk that involves elevation gain.
- Carry plenty of water and snacks, and don't forget to consume them! As we age, our "thirst sensors" don't function as reliably as they should, so we have to remind ourselves to rehydrate regularly, even if we don't feel thirsty.
- After warming up or walking for a bit, take a short break to stretch your legs and back. This will make you feel better and may reduce the risk of injury.
- Bring a basic first-aid kit that includes your medications, ibuprofen, aspirin, antacids, antihistamines, and adhesive bandages. You'll want to beef this up with splint materials and other items for longer hikes or heading off-trail (see Chapter 11: The Avian Survival Kit for more information).
- Always check the weather before you head out so that you know

what kind of clothing to wear and what kind of conditions you may face.

## Wheelchairs and Walkers

If you use a walker or a wheelchair, you will face additional challenges but, hopefully, know your needs, abilities, and limitations. I have been truly impressed by the efforts across the country to create more accessible trails and provide detailed information to people with disabilities. I already mentioned the spectacular new wheelchair-accessible canopy walk built by Houston Audubon at High Island's Smith Oaks nature site, but I have seen similar walkways at nature areas across the country. One especially handy resource on the Birdability website that I mentioned earlier is a crowdsourced map that reviews accessible birding sites around the country (see Resources). Anyone can add birding locations to it, and hopefully this will keep growing in usefulness as more people contribute.

But wait! You don't actually have to get out on a trail to bird. Backyard birding is an excellent option for people with limited mobility, especially if you place birdfeeders and water features in your yard. So is just setting up a chair at a campground, park, or other outdoor spot. Grab yourself a beverage and a good book (preferably this one), and let the birds come to you. You may be astonished how many species drop by.

Car birding is another choice used by people of *all* abilities. Some of Braden's and my favorite excursions involve driving loops through natural areas in Montana, where the best way to spot grassland birds and waterfowl is to drive slowly along back roads and wildlife refuges. We have found and enjoyed similar routes in many parts of the country.

## Don't Ignore Your Other Workouts

Perhaps it's obvious, but I want to emphasize that, by itself, birding usually won't serve as a comprehensive exercise regime. Typically, birders move at a slow, methodical pace, stopping frequently to try to spot or identify birds, and we often don't cover too much ground or get our hearts pumping. Still, birding certainly adds to any exercise that you are already doing, and you can even combine it with other activities such as walking your dog, cage fighting, or for those of Scotch ancestry, tossing the caber.

The bottom line is that unless you have the most severe of disabilities or situations, birding is not only possible, it is likely to help—not hinder—your body's overall health.

CHAPTER 20

# The Birding Brain, or What Was This Chapter About Again?

Just as our bodies play a pivotal role in our ability to find and detect birds, our brains control our capacity to identify and learn about them. Some people just have "birdier" brains than others and are able to absorb and remember key details better—whether that is the color or shape of a bird, its various vocalizations, or what it looks like flying. I'd like to go on record that I deeply resent such people, but many of these exceptional abilities must be shaped when we are young.

When it comes to learning birdsong, for example, I've noticed that many people who excel at "ear birding" had strong musical backgrounds as youths. This is true for both my wife and son, several ornithology professors I know, and Hear Birds Again app creator Harold Mills, who played piano as a child. Since so much of our brain development occurs in our early years, their neural circuitry may be better built to recognize and learn the patterns, frequencies, and other nuances of bird vocalizations.

Even if my ears were not damaged, I suspect my brain functions a little worse than average at learning new bird vocalizations—unless the birds happen to be singing twelve-bar blues! When I was a junior in college, I decided to take music appreciation as an easy, fun elective, and every week

we had to listen to and learn new classical pieces by different composers. It was the only class I failed in my college career. I don't think I put in less effort than others. I just didn't retain what I was hearing. That same lack of retention now applies to most bird songs, and as a result I have come to accept that ear birding is just not something I'm ever going to excel at.

I am much better at learning birds by their appearance—and that's probably no accident, either. I asked Bruce Byers, the biologist I discussed in Chapter 7: Sounding Out Birdsong, why bird vocalizations are so difficult to learn. As he explained, humans are generally more visually oriented. We often remember what we *see* better than what we hear.

This may explain why some people learn birdsong better with the aid of sonograms (or spectrograms)—the little graphic recordings of bird songs I also discussed earlier. "Making a sonogram or a picture of sound," Byers says, "makes it really easy for a human observer to pick out a bird syllable and to see that a song is made up of syllables."

The sad news is that whatever your natural abilities, age is likely to erode them. As I've mentioned several times, it's important not to "rage at the machine," but to try to accept where you are so that you can figure out how best to proceed.

On the other hand, you can take great satisfaction in the fact that struggling to learn to identify birds both visually and by sound cannot help but maintain, and even improve, your current brain function. I haven't delved into the research but would bet that pursuing bird study beats the hell out of doing crossword puzzles and other word games when it comes to keeping your brain sharp and active.

## Visual–Aural Connections

Regardless of our age, a major key to learning *any* kind of bird attribute is repetition. In my own case, just looking at an illustration in *Sibley* or a photo on Merlin will not teach me a bird. I have to both study it *and* get out in the field over and over to really come to know it. In fact, seeing a bird in the field often imprints it much better on my brain than a photo or illustration. Byers says the same about learning a bird's song: "For me to really fix a new bird song in my mind, I have to see the bird sing it. I can hear a yellow warbler a million times but what really fixes it is using my binoculars to hear it and see it at the same time."

Why would that be? It could be that when you're out in the field you are picking up more clues, such as habitat and behavior, that add to a success-ful identification. It could also be that your brain is struggling harder to learn and thus forming more neural connections than if you are passively looking at an illustration.

When you can't get out in the field, quizzes are a great way to practice and strengthen those connections. One of the things I miss most about Braden going away to college is how, ahead of any birding expedition, he and I use to make quizzes for each other by opening a bunch of photos on the internet. Fortunately, the eBird website has come to the rescue with quizzes I can tailor to my date and location. I'll go into this in greater detail in Chapter 22: eBird: The Birder's Lifeline.

# PART VI

# THE ADVANCED BIRDING ARSENAL

*Anytime you find someone more successful than you are, especially when you're both birding—you know they're doing something that you aren't.*
*—Malcolm X*

## CHAPTER 21

# Tackling Difficult Birds, Group by Group

Although some of the previous topics I've covered are fairly sophisticated, they pretty much fall into the category of basic birding. As birding continues to take hold of your being, however, you will find yourself stretching into areas you never imagined, and that's what we're going to cover in this section, beginning with advanced bird identification.

Even in your first year of birding, you will observe that your ability to identify different species will swell with confidence—only to plunge like the stock market on Black Monday. Do not be alarmed. This will happen over and over, crushing your soul time after time. Each time you think you've mastered a particular bird or group of birds, the birds themselves will casually defecate all over what you think you know.

This occurred to me most recently with warblers. Like most people, I learned my warbler identifications by studying photos and illustrations of bright, bold males in breeding season. There are so many warbler species that this presented a tough enough challenge, but I finally pinned down most of them and was feeling pretty smug about it. Imagine my dismay when I got out into the field and discovered two horrifying facts: first, roughly half of all warblers are females with different coloration than their male counterparts, and second, field markings for both males and

females often change dramatically during fall and winter,
rendering them much more
difficult to identify.

The duck situation mim-
ics the warbler situation, as
breeding male ducks generally display glorious bold color
patterns while females and
"off season" ducks merge into
a morass of confusion and befuddlement. As difficult as these two groups
are, however, they barely merit a mention compared to some other bird
groups that will continue to (a) challenge or (b) bedevil you your entire
birding life. A short list includes the sparrows, gulls, shorebirds, hawks,
flycatchers, and pelagic birds—which I'm not even going to discuss because
the main time you'll encounter pelagics is out on an ocean cruise, and you'll
be too busy throwing up to look for birds anyway. For the other five groups,
though, are there any ways to really learn the different species?

There are. Several, in fact.

One of the most effective ways to learn any difficult group is to utilize
a birder's version of the scientific method. Instead of proving what a bird
*is*, it's often easier to prove what it *is not*. I provided a good example of
this in Chapter 6: Braving Bird Identification where I showed how one
might identify a Hermit Thrush by ruling out American Robin, Swainson's,
and other thrush species. Subconsciously, we birders employ this "ruling
out" strategy all the time, but it especially comes in handy for tough bird
groups.

It bears repeating that a big part of this process of elimination is to
pay close attention to where a bird is located. Often, certain species will
be found only in certain habitats. By realizing "Oh, I'm in a high-altitude
conifer forest, not down by the river," you can eliminate a lot of species
and narrow your choices considerably. Knowing a bird's seasonal range

also proves invaluable. If you see a soaring hawk in summer instead of winter, that greatly restricts which species it can be. Finally, if you've got an ear for them—or gain both proficiency and discretion with Sound ID— bird vocalizations can almost always clinch the deal.

As indicated elsewhere in this book, a great way to fast-track your skills is to go out with birders who are more knowledgeable and experienced than you are. Advanced birders often zero in on key details and clues that you won't find in any field guides, and this is especially true for the tougher bird groups. With that short introduction, let's explore real-world examples by taking a look at some of the toughest bird groups in North America, both to complain about them and see if there are any specific strategies to learning them.

## Sparrows

With about forty-five American species, sparrows intimidate most beginning birders. This is not only because they are literally Little Brown Birds, but because they constantly flit around in the brush or dive into the grass, rendering them difficult to see. The good news is that some sparrows really stand out, including Dark-eyed Juncos, Black-throated Sparrows, White-throated Sparrows, six kinds of towhees, and others.

If you can actually get your binoculars on them, you'll discover that even all of the "brownish" species often have quite distinctive markings. Savannah Sparrows usually sport little yellow patches above and in front of their eyes, for instance, while Lark Sparrows have bold, almost Aztec-style facial patterns.

Habitat knowledge and seasonal distribution unlock the answer to many sparrow species. Lincoln's Sparrows and White-crowned Sparrows, for example, both can have breeding territories at high elevations, but Lincoln's favors boggy areas with moss, willows, and thick shrubs. White-crowneds tend toward drier areas with grass and bare ground, but also containing thick shrubs and bordered by tall trees. American Tree Sparrows look extremely similar to Field and Chipping Sparrows, but while the former appear mostly in winter in the Lower 48, the latter two species are predominantly summer or year-round birds.

Generally, the first thing I do when I see a sparrow is make sure it's not a Song Sparrow or an invasive House Sparrow. These are the two most common sparrows I'm likely to encounter, and once I eliminate them, it dramatically narrows down my choices. Still, mastering all of the sparrows takes a keen eye.

Once again, patience and persistence are the key—advice that applies to every other group below.

## Gulls

In some ways, gulls are even harder than sparrows. When I'm trying to ID a gull, I look at (generally in order) bill color and markings, leg color, eye color, wing color, body size, and tail markings. For an adult gull, these will usually give you the ID answer. Gulls, however, don't want to make it that easy for you! To make your life more difficult, most mature gulls look radically different than they do in first-, second-, and sometimes third-year plumage. Not only that but those early plumages look almost the same for many different species: generally brownish, mottled, and nondescript.

To further antagonize you, many gulls throw in different plumages between breeding and nonbreeding seasons. This is particularly evident for the group of "black-headed gulls," which lose most of their black head feathers in winter. If that's not galling—or should I say *gulling*—enough, gull species hybridize (crossbreed) like crazy, making it almost impossible

to figure out what you're really looking at!

Probably the most useful thing to do as a beginning birder is study range maps to figure out which gulls are likely to be in your particular location and season. Here in Montana in winter (when I'm writing this), that generally narrows things down to Ring-billed, Herring, and perhaps California Gulls.

Others *can* show up, but these are the three I start with, and that makes my job a lot easier. Ring-billed Gulls, for instance, are the only adult gulls around here with a thick black band circling the tip of the bill. Herring and California Gulls can both have a red spot at the tip of the bill, but California Gulls usually also sport a tiny bit of black. The tiebreakers for these two are eye and leg colors. Herring Gulls have large yellow eyes and pinkish legs while California Gulls have smaller, darker eyes and yellow legs. Herring Gulls are also the largest of the three, something I pay attention to when several gulls are standing side by side. With practice, you'll come up with your own tiebreakers for the gulls in your area.

One final gull note: there is no such thing as a *seagull*, so exorcise that word from your vocabulary!

## Shorebirds

Just saying the word "shorebird" renders me almost apoplectic. That's how hard many of these birds can be to ID. So let's start with some that are actually *very easy* to identify. Godwits, oystercatchers, avocets, Long-billed Curlews, Surfbirds, Wilson's Snipes are all fairly large, distinctive species that are a joy to identify and observe, both because they have obvious features and because they are often breathtakingly beautiful.

Where it gets tough is with plovers and sandpipers. The three main smallish sandpipers, or "peeps"—the Western, Semipalmated, and Least Sandpipers—are notoriously difficult to pin down. First, they are all about the same size, about six to six and a half inches long. Their colors often overlap, but also vary greatly between locations and seasons. And all three run around frantically probing sand or mud. What to do?

As with other difficult species, you need to examine multiple ID features. The first thing Braden and I do is look at leg color because Least Sandpipers have yellow legs while Western and "Semis" have black. But because of where they live and feed, a Least's yellow legs are often covered in mud, eliminating that easy fix. So then we move on to the bill length. In general, Westerns have longer, curving bills—but not always, and Semis and Leasts can also occasionally have long, curving bills. That takes us to overall color, with Leasts generally having darker, more brown feathers in all seasons, but again, there is huge variation and overlap to the point that for me, colors are almost meaningless.

The bottom line is that even experts can't tell some peeps apart, so don't feel bad if you struggle with them. Fortunately, other sandpipers are a bit easier to identify.

## Hawks

Two things make hawks difficult. One is that you usually see them perched on telephone poles when you are zipping past at seventy-five miles an hour, making it tough to identify them without crashing your car and killing all of your loved ones. Second, hawks come in several different color morphs, or variations, rendering them even more challenging to pin down.

There are generally two categories of hawks. Accipiters are fast, flashy hawks that are almost falcon-like and specialize in flying through forests chasing other birds. They include, from smallest to largest, Sharp-shinned Hawks, Cooper's Hawks, and Northern Goshawks. Then there are the

buteos—the large, soaring hawks you are most likely to see circling slowly in the sky or sitting on manmade objects. Buteos are probably the first hawks you'll start paying attention to, so let's stick with them.

One of the most useful things to do with buteos, as with gulls, is to study range maps to figure out which varieties are even possible near you. Our most common hawk, the Red-tailed, lives almost throughout North America but comes in a huge variety of color morphs. If it's flying, the bird's red tail can give it away, but even that disappears in some varieties and in juveniles. Still, if you see a big brown hawk with a dark head and belly band, it's probably going to be a Red-tailed.

You may also live in or visit a place with Red-shouldered Hawks, easily distinguished by their repeating *kee-a, kee-a, kee-a, kee-a* call, and smallish Broad-winged Hawks that have bold black and white bands on their tails. Neither of these are common where I live, but range maps tell me that in summer we *do* have both Swainson's and Ferruginous Hawks. So if I see a hawk on a telephone pole and determine it is not a Red-tailed, I next look for the white chin of a Swainson's or the pale, often streaky head of a Ferruginous.

In winter, these two species fly south to be replaced by Rough-legged Hawks moving down from the Arctic. Most of you in middle and northern states also have Rough-leggeds in winter, and they are easy to ID by their whitish heads and, in flight, a distinct dark patch on the underside of each wing. Most of our other buteos are also very distinctive and can be found only in certain, restricted parts of the country. A quick look through your field guide maps will show what's possible near you.

## Flycatchers

Okay, I really don't want to talk about flycatchers, and the reasons will become clear once you start trying to ID them in the field. To begin, many, *many* types of birds fall under the loose heading of "flycatchers." *Sibley* lists forty-four species of flycatchers in two different families, the Tyrannidae and Tityridae. In addition to birds with the actual name "flycatcher," this category includes pewees, phoebes, kingbirds, tyrannulets, kiskadees, and becards.

A few flycatchers have bold, distinct markings that make them easy to pick out. These include both Black and Say's Phoebes, Great Crested Flycatcher, Great Kiskadee, Sulphur-bellied Flycatcher, Eastern Kingbird, Vermilion Flycatcher, Scissor-tailed Flycatcher, and one or two more. That still leaves quite a few species that will rear their all-too-similar heads, especially pewees, a lot of kingbirds, and (ominous music playing) the birds in the genus *Empidonax*.

The approach for dealing with these "problematic" birds mirrors strategies we've already covered but is even harder to execute. If your hearing still works, first listen for the song of the bird. This won't be the beautiful, lilting symphony that emanates from, say, an oriole or meadowlark. Two flycatcher songs that stand out for me are the loud, descending *PHSHEeeeew* of the wood-pewees and the clear song of the Western Flycatcher (until recently, known as the Cordilleran Flycatcher) that *Sibley* describes as a "rising *tweep*." But those are the easy ones.

Most "empids," or flycatchers in the genus *Empidonax*, have quiet, almost scratchy songs that I usually miss entirely, even with my hearing aids cranked up. Earlier I mentioned the *FITZ-pew* of the Willow Flycatcher. The Least Flycatcher makes a short *che-BEK* call. I won't attempt to describe the other empid songs because I almost never hear them. If you *do* still have functional ears, though, flycatcher songs are going to be hands-down your best way to ID different species—especially in spring.

Don't be shy about using Merlin's Sound ID feature. Not only will it alert you to when a flycatcher is in the area, it seems pretty good at correctly identifying the song to species.

As with other tough bird groups, range maps and habitats are useful for identifying flycatchers. Empids, for example—Western, Willow, Alder, Least, Hammond's, Dusky, Acadian, Yellow-bellied, Buff-breasted, and Gray Flycatchers—range across the country, often overlapping (especially in migration), and pretty much look identical. Whew, right? Or should I say *Fitz-whew*?

Anyway, when faced with one of these birds, the first thing I do is go home and make myself some hot chocolate. Just kidding. The *first* thing I do is glance at the range maps in my field guide to know which species I can throw out. A quick look through *Sibley* reveals that Alder, Acadian, Yellow-bellied, Buff-breasted, and Gray are either rare or don't live anywhere near me, so that narrows my list down to five that do: Western, Willow, Least, Hammond's, and Dusky. And while some experts *claim* they can tell these apart by their physical features, the overlap in their appearance is so great that, really, I have to go to my final, and perhaps most useful, tool: habitats.

The five empids I list above tend to live in pretty well-defined areas:

- **Western:** found mostly in shady forests next to streams and steep-sided banks or cliffs
- **Willow:** almost always found in wet riparian areas dominated by willows and cattails
- **Hammond's:** hunts high in the trees of mature coniferous forests
- **Dusky:** prefers brushier areas within open forests
- **Least:** almost anywhere in deciduous forests, but often near streams

Knowing these habitat parameters gives me perhaps the best idea of which empid I might be looking at—but it doesn't put me, ahem, out of the woods. There is still significant habitat overlap between Hammond's and Dusky Flycatchers, and between Least and Western Flycatch-

# Lumpers and Splitters

As if bird identification weren't challenging enough, scientists enjoy frustrating birders even more by frequently lumping species together or, more commonly, dividing species into *other* species. To wit, the Pacific-slope and Cordilleran Flycatchers used to be grouped into one species, the Western Flycatcher. Apparently, this made the bird too easy for birders to identify, so budding ornithologists succeeded in dividing them into two separate species. Even to experts, however, the two species are virtually identical, and genetic analysis often reveals "hybridization," which, looking at it another way, could simply mean that they aren't two separate species after all.

The only convenient thing about this split was that experts created a pretty clear geographic boundary between the two—at least in the US. If you were in the Rocky Mountains, you *almost* always would be looking at a Cordilleran Flycatcher. If you were farther west, the Pacific-slope was *almost* always your bird.

But not so fast! Just in the last year, the Taxonomic Powers That Be had a change of heart, and it looks as if they have decided to rejoin Cordilleran and Pacific-slope Flycatchers into one species—the Western Flycatcher.

Similar taxonomic upheavals have occurred with crossbills, juncos, murrelets, meadowlarks, and other species, and many more may be on the way. Recent studies suggest that the true number of bird species may be close to 18,000 instead of the 11,000 or so that have been recognized of late. For now, you probably don't have to worry about this. Just don't be surprised if you suddenly gain or lose a species on your life list!

ers, casting their IDs in doubt. Experienced bird banders claim that the Dusky does indeed have a slightly darker, "duskier" appearance than Hammond's, and as I mentioned before, others claim they can distinguish empid species by sight. Unless someone has been intensely studying these birds for at least five or ten years, however, call me very, *very* skeptical.

Which brings us full circle back to the most reliable feature you can use to distinguish many flycatcher species: the bird's song. With flycatchers as with many other birds, no one thing is probably going to cinch the ID. Instead, you will want to rely on as many ID features and tools as you can.

My final words on the subject: good luck!

CHAPTER 22

# eBird: The Birder's Lifeline

You've heard the hype. You've seen the Super Bowl halftime show. You've read the reviews. Now, at last, it's time to officially unveil it. The program you've all been waiting for . . .

eBird.

Okay, I know that earlier in the book I said that you really need only binoculars and a field guide to begin birding, but eBird is a tool that has become indispensable to almost every birder I know who has been birding for any length of time. So if you think you can handle it, it's time to take a deep dive into this powerful program.

Braden and I may be the last crop of birders who began birding without using eBird, but once we plunged in, it became as vital as jelly is to peanut butter, or a remote is to a television, or—I'm struggling to find suitable similes here, so let's just say that for most experienced birders, eBird is *really, really* important.

eBird is a website and app that is managed by the Cornell Lab of Ornithology but has been a collaborative effort of dozens of US and international partners. It was conceived as a way to access the wealth of data collected by ordinary birders around the globe in real time. But these eBird folks were so frickin' smart. They quickly figured out that if they wanted access to everyone's data, they'd better make their program useful *and* fun for the ordinary birder. As a result, they offered eBird for free and turned it into the ultimate tool to quickly and easily record and store your sightings.

It worked.

In recent years, "eBirders" have contributed more than 1.4 *billion* bird observations to the database! In just one year, for example, they—I really should say "we" since I am one of them—submitted 16.5 million checklists along with 10.5 million photos and 389,200 audio recordings. During the year, more than 110,000 new birders also signed up and started submitting, undoubtedly making eBird one of the largest, if not *the* largest, community-science efforts in the world. eBird observations have allowed us to vastly increase our understanding of bird populations, distributions, and movements and helped scientists formulate and execute strategies for protecting birds.

But for the individual birder, eBird goes far beyond just recording data. Once you submit your data via the app or website, you can access it in innumerable ways. You can track your day, month, year, and life lists, and pull up every observation of a species you've ever made. You can compare your observations at particular locations during different years and seasons. You can get a list of birds you still need for an area in the order of how commonly each is observed. But wait, there's more.

If you're looking for a good place to bird, eBird can display thousands of nearby hotspots and show what's been observed at each one recently. It also gives you bar charts and species maps to learn which times of year various species are most likely to occur. Similarly, if you want to find a particular species, you can see where and when it has been sighted near you—and sign up for email alerts to inform you when rarities and birds you need for your life list or other lists show up at local, state, and national locations.

Want to learn more about a bird? Simply click on that species and eBird connects you to an information page that provides ID tips, life history information, photos, song recordings, and range maps. For you competitive types, eBird will rank you against other birders in your county, state, or country for a given time period. As mentioned earlier, it will even create tailor-made photo and sound quizzes to help you sharpen your skills. Before taking a closer look at some of these features, however, let's get you set up.

## Setting Up eBIRD

To use eBird you will need to create a free account. I recommend doing this on a computer at the eBird.org website, as it will be easier on the eyes and fingers than doing it on your phone. However, once you have your account, dig out your smartphone and download the free eBird app from the app store. Log in with the credentials you used to set up your account, and you're ready to begin.

Note that the eBird website and the eBird app work hand-in-hand, and you will undoubtedly find yourself using both of them extensively. To wit, many of eBird's cooler features are available exclusively on the website, while the app makes it much easier to record your observations in real time while out in the field. (Also note: websites and, especially, apps are constantly being updated, so some of the directions and tips here may evolve and look a bit different when you sign up.)

At the heart of both website and app, however, is the eBird checklist.

## The eBIRD Checklist

When Braden and I began birding, we kept our checklists by hand. Every time we went out, we'd carry a notepad with us and scribble down every species we saw using a pen or pencil. Although this appealed to a simpler time in human history and was rather quaint, it was also a huge pain in the ass. Rain and fog damaged our notepads. We were constantly misplacing or losing them or our writing implements. Most critically, keeping up with what we saw proved a constant challenge.

The eBird checklist changed all that. It allowed us to quickly and efficiently record the birds we saw no matter where we were or under what conditions. Best of all, it was incredibly easy to use—and will be for you too.

The next time you go somewhere to bird, simply pull out your phone and open the app, then tap Start Checklist. A list of possible birds based on your general location will appear, but you should enter your *specific* location by tapping the little orange balloon with a plus sign in it in the upper right-hand corner and choosing from the options that appear.

When you ID a bird, find that species on the checklist by either scrolling through it or typing the bird's common name, scientific name, or four-letter banding code into the search bar. Once you locate your bird, enter the number of individuals you saw, tap the species name to confirm, and keep birding. By default, the app uses GPS coordinates to record your time and the actual route you take, but if you don't want to use this feature or need to conserve your phone's battery life, you can disable it before you hit Start Checklist. When you have finished birding in a location, hit Stop, check over your list and, if you are birding with other eBird users, share your list with them. Then tap Submit, and that's it.

On the app version you can edit or revise your list to a certain degree, but to make more substantial changes or add photos and sound recordings, you (for now) have to use the web version of the program. As I mentioned, the two versions work very much in tandem, and Braden and I find ourselves frequently switching back and forth between them.

# birdSTAT

One nice feature of eBird is that you can download all your data into a .cvs file—a simple compressed data file that software developers and birding enthusiasts have taken advantage of in finding cool new ways to utilize the program. Braden recently turned me on to a wonderful web-based program called birdSTAT (birdSTAT.com), created by Zak Pohlen, a wildlife biologist with a passion for birds and citizen science.

birdSTAT presents your personalized data statistically, graphically, and even geographically. To use it, go to the My eBird tab of the eBird website. Download your data to your computer, then go to the birdSTAT website and upload that data file using the Browse option. *Shazam!* Just like that, your lifelong birding information will appear in a plethora of entertaining formats.

If you're like me, you'll be amazed at the statistics laid out in front of you. I just uploaded my latest info and learned that in my eBirding career I have spent 2,247 hours recording 380,008 individual birds from 114 families. Not surprisingly, the most checklists (225) I have submitted from any one location are from my yard. I've seen the most species (135) at a spot called the Fort Missoula Gravel Quarry. The total hours I've spent birding using eBird has been remarkably consistent at about 350 hours per year for five years. The bird showing up most frequently on my checklists? American Robin, with 981 records, while the honor for the most individuals of any one species belong to the American Coot with 53,962 birds recorded—though there was one hiding behind a cattail, so the true number may be 53,963.

Beyond the above types of info, you'll find graphs, maps, and even a calendar showing the number of species you've seen each day. Perhaps the most amazing thing about birdSTAT is that Zak Pohlen created it all on his own time and dime. If you enjoy using birdSTAT—and I know you will—please consider sending him a donation through the website so he can continue his work and keep the servers running.

## Finding Birding Locations

One of the outstanding features of eBird is that it can help you find great places to bird. This can be done on the phone app, but is easier to do on the website before you head out. Simply jump on eBird, click the Explore tab, and then click on Explore Hotspots. A world map will appear, and in the search window, type in the name of your town, county, or state. Voilá! A map of your locale will pop up with tiny colored balloons indicating the birding hotspots in your vicinity. Colors with longer wavelengths (orange and red—sorry, couldn't resist using my physics) indicate that more species have been found at that spot while blue and gray balloons boast fewer species. Click on any of these balloons and hit View Details and a list will appear of all the species seen there, the most recent birds first. Look at the dark blue bar across the top of the page and you'll see that you can parse this list in different ways by date and year, and this will help give you a preview of what you might see *now* when you're about to visit the site. You can also call up bar charts showing when each species is most likely to be present throughout the year—a feature I use a lot.

## Bird Quizzes

As I've hinted at, one of my favorite features of eBird is its ability to generate quizzes for almost any birding place and time of year. Just sign in to the web version of eBird, click the Explore tab and find the Photo + Sound Quiz button. Once you've started the quiz, you'll be able to customize your desired location and date. The program will pull photos and recordings randomly from millions of eBird checklists to create a multiple-choice test.

In addition to improving your skills in "virtual real world" conditions, these quizzes are a lot of fun and give you something to do when you've watched the season's last episode of your favorite streaming show.

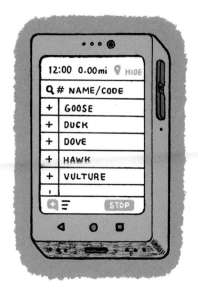

## Assuming the Throne

I also mentioned earlier that, in addition to the above useful features, eBird can help you tap into your competitive streak. A fun way to motivate yourself to get out birding is to try to become king or queen of a particular spot. When you call up a birding hotspot on the web version of eBird, it gives you top-ten lists of people who have seen the most species at that hotspot and of those with the greatest number of recorded checklists. I pointed this out to my friend Roger when he first got into birding, and he quickly set about "conquering" Cerrito Vista Park near his home in the Bay Area. To become king, he began birding the spot several times a week, and the species mounted up until he was able to dethrone the previous monarch. Unfortunately, once Roger and his wife moved to Oregon, several birder barbarians mounted a coup and overthrew him by finding even more birds.

I conducted a similar assault on the Missoula Cemetery. During the COVID-19 pandemic, I wanted to start birding more by bicycle, and the cemetery happened to be the right distance away to give me a good workout. I didn't know how many birds I would discover there, but the place ended up surprising me over and over. Soon I had dethroned the previous species king and, over the course of a year, amassed what I hope will be an insurmountable total.

Putting in this kind of time, of course, greatly sharpens your ID skills and allows you to learn the habits and seasonality of local avifauna.

Migration is an especially fun time to bird your favorite places because you can make valuable contributions to the birding databases kept by Cornell Lab. In any given place, birds show up that you might never expect, and the fact that *you* saw one in Location A on a particular date provides key information to scientists and other birders. My very first time at the Missoula Cemetery, I saw two Brown Creepers—a species I haven't seen there since. Over the next couple of years, I had a host of other unexpected encounters with Cordilleran (Western) Flycatchers, MacGillivray's Warblers, American Pipits, Common Redpolls, White-throated Sparrows—even, on my most recent visit, a Peregrine Falcon!

As the late, great Tom Petty recognized, "It's good to be king."

## eCREATIVITY

eBird developers continue to add new features all the time, and birders, in turn, continue to find creative ways to use it. Just the other night, I visited with folks from a nearby Audubon chapter that decided to do a group Big Year for their county (see Chapter 25: Big Years and Other Insane Ideas). Members of the group share their birding lists via a centralized eBird account to track how many total species the entire group has seen so far. I'm not in the group, but I can't wait to see their year-end total! Birders create other intriguing eBird challenges all the time. eBird also creates "eBirder of the Month" and other challenges to help you improve your skills and test your mettle against other birders.

If it all sounds too easy, well, it is. eBird is not only a huge amount of fun to work with and explore, it relieves you of a ton of burdensome record-keeping. And that frees you up to do what you really want to do: go birding.

## CHAPTER 23

# The Spotting Scope: Birding's Super Tool

When Braden and I first started birding, we kind of snickered at people who lugged around spotting scopes—basically little telescopes, usually mounted on tripods, that birders, hunters, and spies use to observe distant animals and double agents. To us, the scopes seemed like a major pain to deal with, and their owners seemed doggedly compelled to set them up whether they were looking at a distant circling raptor or a pigeon perched across the street. Since then, we've come to appreciate the great utility of spotting scopes and how they enhance our birding experience. Without one, we have almost no chance at identifying shorebirds in many circumstances. We learned that a scope also comes in handy for all kinds of other situations, ranging from IDing a Prairie Falcon perched on a telephone pole to distinguishing between Cedar and Bohemian Waxwings on a cold winter's day. If you get a flat tire on a steep hill, it's also handy to wedge the scope under your rear tire so your car won't roll backward.

We bought our first scope for a couple hundred bucks—and may as well have thrown the money into the gutter. Sure, it was better than nothing, but the images were dim and fuzzy, and often weren't a great improvement over our binoculars. More recently, I shelled out significantly more for a much higher-quality and better-made scope and have been delighted with the crisp, well-lit images it produces. Still, that doesn't make me a scope

# Don't Forget the Tripod!

An important thing to remember when buying a spotting scope is that you're also going to need a tripod—unless you plan to always balance your "mini-telescope" on a nearby object such as a fencepost, a sheep, or your grandchild's head. *Don't scrimp on the tripod!* Many tripods are flimsy and shake even in mild wind conditions. This renders all the money you spent on the scope practically pointless. Instead, look for something beefy enough to act as a solid platform for your optics.

Gazillions of tripods are on the market, and they can be outfitted with at least four or five types of heads—the gizmo at the top of the tripod that attaches to your scope or camera. The ones typically used with spotting scopes are "pan and tilt" heads and "ball" heads. A pan and tilt head has two different knobs or controls that allow you to move the scope in two different planes. Honestly, I don't know why so many people like these. By the time I've fiddled with these knobs—and the knob or ring that swivels the tripod platform to the left and right—I more often than not have lost the bird that I'm trying to zoom in on, and have started contemplating where the nearest bakery might be located.

I much prefer a tripod with a ball head. This allows me to swivel the scope in any or all directions at once, and all I have to do is loosen or tighten a single knob. I've been very happy with my Alta Pro 263AT ball head tripod. It is a bit heavy, but it provides the stability and ease of use that I need. It's perfect for car birding, but I also can easily carry it along on hikes of up to a mile or so.

Glenn Olsen, of GO Birding Ecotours, reports that he has several tripods, but says that he uses one more than the others because it's sturdy, easy to use, and is fairly lightweight for its large size. For him, it's important that a tripod has a wide "stance," or legs that spread out farther to keep the tripod steady. "I have twice had a tripod with a narrow spread get blown over by big gusts of wind," he cautions.

Expect to pay a few hundred dollars for a good tripod, so shop around, and if you can, try out other birders' rigs—including carrying them around with a scope attached. Also note that if you do a lot of car birding, compact spotting scope mounts are available that attach to your car window. This is an especially great tool for people with mobility issues, but I have seen plenty of other birders use them as well. If you're fortunate enough to live in a bigger city with a good photography, optics, or birding store, be sure to take advantage of it to test the full range of scopes, tripods, and other accessories. Online retailers are usually able to accept products for a full refund or exchange if you need to test a few styles, but make sure you know before you buy.

expert, so for a big-picture view, I turn to veteran birder and birding guide Glenn Olsen, owner of GO Birding Ecotours.

I first met Olsen in Houston, where I was speaking at a fundraiser for Houston Audubon, and he determinedly helped me chase down Brown Boobies, Red-cockaded Woodpeckers, and Limpkins so that I could break my former Big Year record. And yes, he carried a scope wherever we went.

"Scopes are wonderful optics for birding, second only to binoculars," he explains. "I find scopes most beneficial for watching shorebirds, marsh birds, and birds perched at a distance. Also, a scope can be beneficial when observing migrating hawks." He cautions, though, that scopes are generally more trouble than they're worth when viewing songbirds and other small birds that move around a lot.

Olsen especially recommends scopes for those unable to hold binoculars. "Some birders have excessive trembling of the hands or are not able to hold binoculars steady for various reasons," he says. "If image-stabilized binoculars do not compensate for the issue, oftentimes a scope will." For these situations, he suggests a scope with 10 to 20 power magnification (lower than most scopes) and a 40 to 60mm objective lens diameter. This size is small and lightweight and easily used.

Scopes come in both "straight" and "angled" models, and Olsen, like myself, prefers angled so that we don't have to raise the scope as high to see through it. An even more valuable aspect, according to Olsen, is that angled scopes come with a small knob that when loosened allows you to rotate the scope tube about 170 degrees horizontally. "'This feature allows me to set the tripod and scope height so that it is comfortable and easy for me to use, but also rotate the scope for individuals who are shorter or in wheelchairs."

As far as what kind of raw optical firepower to buy, I prefer one with a larger objective lens of 85mm, which lets in more light and generates a better image at higher magnification, but this comes with more weight to lug around. Olsen and many other birders prefer a 20–60 power (the eyepiece zooms from 20 to 60X magnification) scope with a 60mm objective lens, which offers a great balance of weight, quality optics, and easy handling.

And that leads to the obvious question: which brand and scope to buy?

Olsen has an older model 20 X 60 power 80mm objective lens Zeiss that he uses for local trips, but finds it too cumbersome to fly with. For those trips he uses a Vortex 20 X 60 power with a 60mm objective lens, adding, "I have had the opportunity to view birds in a wide variety of scopes, and many are quite good and a few are excellent. I think Vortex has the best quality of optics for the price, but I happen to prefer Zeiss for the higher end."

Before buying any scope, Olsen first advocates spending the big bucks on an excellent pair of binoculars. If, after that, you still find yourself in situations where you want a scope, and you can afford one, it's a great idea to use as many different kinds as you can before settling on one that fits your needs. Different scopes have many different features, including different focusing systems, varying quality optics and construction, and attachments for digiscoping—taking photographs with your phone or camera through the scope. You'll want to check out all of the options.

## CHAPTER 24

# Bird Photography, or How to Spend Your Retirement Savings

I suppose I could have titled this chapter "More Optics," but in my mind a discussion of cameras and photography encompasses an entirely different planet than binoculars and scopes, and deserves to be treated as such. There's a lot to cover here, so you might want to grab a cookie and mug of tea before plunging in.

For many birders, including Braden and me, photographing birds is a key part of the birding experience. Only rarely do I go birding *without* my camera and zoom lens slung over my shoulder, and I'd say about a third of the other birders I meet do the same.

Why?

One reason is that most birders love to share the birds that we see. Plus, decent bird photos can help us identify species. And for some of us, bird pictures are part of careers as professional photographers, journalists, and authors. Perhaps the most compelling reason to take photos, though, is *because it's fun.*

As you might guess, mastering photography and learning about camera equipment can be a lifelong pursuit, and this chapter is intended to give you only an introduction. If photography interests you, I highly recommend taking a beginning photography course online or locally. Also, many accomplished photographers have written excellent books on bird photography, and with a few simple internet searches, you'll find tremendous resources available on YouTube, various blogs, and even camera manufacturer and store websites. Before you pursue all that, however, let's broach some photography fundamentals.

## The, Ahem, Big Picture

In my humble opinion, the best way to get started taking bird photos is to grab whatever camera you have and go out there and try to take some pictures. This will quickly enlighten you with several valuable lessons:

- Your camera probably sucks at taking bird pictures.
- Birds are incredibly difficult to photograph.
- You really need to learn more about photography.

Believe me, these are essential lessons, because they will either motivate you to get more serious about bird photography, or convince you to skip photography altogether and focus on simply enjoying birds. Either decision is perfectly okay, but in case you want to get serious, let's explore these lessons in more depth.

Unless you are already an experienced photographer, chances are that your camera equipment is *not* up to the task of getting good bird photographs. What do I mean by "good"? Well, beauty is in the eye of the photographer, but I consider a good bird photo to be one that is well lit, sharp (in focus), and zoomed close enough to easily see the subject.

Your first question may be, "Can I get good bird photos with my phone?" Phone cameras, after all, are getting better and better all the time, and eventually, the answer might be yes. For now, though, unless a bird is sitting right in front of you, you probably won't get a really good photo of it with your phone. One exception is using your phone to take photos through a spotting scope. This is called "digiscoping," and some photographers have achieved impressive results with it. Various manufacturers even make special mounts to hold your phone steady and get

the best possible result. In general, however, if you want to get really good bird photos, you will need a camera that has a large electronic sensor and a long telephoto lens.

Digital cameras have different-sized sensors, but the larger the sensor, the more information a camera can capture, creating the potential for a fully detailed, crisp photograph. Cell phones and most point-and-shoot cameras have small sensors, which is one reason it is difficult to get more than a "snapshot-type" image with them. Generally, though, a separate camera body that allows you to attach different kinds of lenses to it comes with a large enough sensor—dubbed a "full frame sensor"—to satisfy your photography potential.

To go along with the camera body, you will need a telephoto lens that magnifies the image enough so that a bird looks fairly close, or large, in the picture frame. This can be either a fixed lens, such as a 400mm lens, or some kind of adjustable lens such as a 100–400mm zoom lens that can move in and out to various magnifications. In my opinion, a 400mm lens is about the smallest magnification that will allow you to get decent bird

# Photography Social

Social media platforms have become especially important to photographers, both as ways to learn about photography and equipment, and to share their work. To get more insight on this, I asked Paul Queneau which sites and other resources he most often goes to. Besides being an outstanding wildlife photographer, Queneau is a professional magazine editor and writer, and he began by recommending several YouTube channels:

- DPReview TV: www.youtube.com/@dpreview
- Tony and Chelsea Northrup: www.youtube.com/@TonyAndChelsea
- Mark Galer (Sony specific): www.youtube.com/@AlphaCreativeSkills

He is also a fan of a number of blogs:

- Digital Photography Review (DPReview): www.dpreview.com
- FStoppers: fstoppers.com
- PetaPixel petapixel.com

Both the YouTube channels and the blogs offer an entertaining mix of technical reviews, photography tips, photography news, and more. On Queneau's recommendation, I scoured the DPReview site to research a lightweight travel camera system and found the reviews enormously helpful. Similar reviews and other information can be easily unearthed with quick searches of Facebook and other platforms.

photos, but my son has taken some terrific shots with a 300mm lens under ideal conditions. Professional wildlife photographers, on the other hand, use lenses up to 600mm or more.

I'll mention specifics later in this chapter, but before that, let's review some basic birding photography tips that will allow you to get better photos no matter what kind of equipment you are using.

## Basic Birding Photography Tips

If you have some experience taking photographs, you'll find that many of the techniques you use for taking good photos of other subjects also apply to birds.

- **The Rule of Thirds:** If you divide a scene into thirds by drawing two lines horizontally and two lines vertically, the most effective position for your subject often lies mostly along one of those lines—or sits at an intersection of two of the lines. In many cases, this creates a more pleasing composition than always having your subject sitting dead center in the middle of the frame.
- **Left to Right Flow and Diagonals:** Most people's eyes naturally scan from left to right, and having a photo's composition lead our eyes in the same direction often creates a better result. For instance, if you have the choice of a bird looking left vs. looking right, right is generally more satisfying. Similarly, if the line of the subject (such as the body of the bird) is positioned diagonally from the upper left to the lower right, or from the lower left to the upper right, this also leads to a more interesting, dynamic composition.
- **Good Lighting:** Well-lit subjects are, of course, far more pleasing to look at than poorly lit ones. Better light also allows a camera's autofocus to create a sharper image. Most photographers consider lighting to be one of the keys to taking great photos.

As useful as such basic concepts are, you'll find that photographing birds also requires additional skills. That's because birds are often far away, moving around a lot, or perched or flying against a bright background. We've already talked about the utility of a zoom lens to bring a bird closer, but what do you do about a bird that is flying or moving around? As in most photography, one of your main goals is to capture your subject in sharp focus, but for birds and other animals, the key is to get the animal's eye or eyes in focus. Here are several ways to achieve this and compensate for other bird photography challenges:

- **Restrict the Active Focal Area of Your Camera:** Most cameras, including smartphone cameras, allow you to choose the part of the photo you want the camera to focus on. On my camera, I can choose a very small focal window—and point that window right at a bird's eye in the viewfinder. This gets the camera to ignore the focus of surrounding areas and prioritize just the most critical part of the subject.

- **Set a Fast Shutter Speed:** Most cameras also allow you to manually choose your shutter speed, or they come with "sports modes" that automatically choose a high shutter speed. A shutter speed basically indicates how quickly a camera takes the photo. Slow shutter speeds allow your subject to move more *while the photo is being taken*, increasing the chances of a blurry photo. If I am photographing birds that are moving around a lot, I set the shutter speed at a fast 1/2000 of a second if there is enough light to do so. For birds that are sitting still, much slower speeds may work, but in general I wouldn't shoot slower than 1/500 of a second. Higher shutter speeds are especially good if you are holding your camera by hand because they compensate for your body movement, increasing the likelihood of a sharp photo.

- **Turn On "Predictive Focus" Mode:** Many cameras come with a setting that tells it to recognize a moving object and predict where it will be when the camera actually takes the photo. This improves the odds of capturing a subject in focus.

- **Overexpose in Backlit or Underlit Conditions:** If you are trying to photograph a bird flying above you against a bright sky or one that is skulking around under a dark bush, it's almost guaranteed that the camera will not choose the correct exposure for your subject. That's because extra light is coming in from all around the bird, leading the camera to pay attention to the wrong part of the picture frame. Fortunately, you can compensate for this error by manually overexposing the picture. *How* you do this depends on the brand and type of camera, but almost all cameras make this possible, and you'll need to take advantage of this feature in order to "see" your bird in backlit and underlit conditions.

- **Take a Lot of Photos:** Because birds move around a lot, the chances you'll get a good shot increase if you take a lot of photos. Often, I just keep my finger pressed down on the shooting button, firing away in burst mode until I've captured thirty or forty frames. This frequently results in at least one or two acceptable photos.

- **Use a Tripod:** Because I'm lazy, I usually take "handheld" photographs. When I really want a good photo, though, and I feel confident a bird isn't going anywhere, I break out a tripod and attach my camera to it. This provides a much more stable platform, reduces camera shake, and greatly increases the chances I'll get a sharp, crisp shot.

- **One Final Note:** check your camera settings *before* you try to take any photo. I can't tell you how many times I've been firing away at a bird, only to discover that my camera was set at a slow shutter speed and my dozens of photos turned out blurry.

## Packages and Brands

With some photography basics under our belts, let's talk a little more about what to buy. Unfortunately, camera equipment can be extremely expensive, so if you have limited means or aren't that picky, stick with your phone or borrow a camera from a friend or family member. If you can afford to explore bird photography further, look for a basic package with a decent camera body and zoom lens at a price that's comfortable for you. When I was just getting into digital photography, I bought a couple of these types of packages, and they taught me a lot about digital photography basics. The problems? The equipment often didn't stand up to getting

# Used Equipment and Renting

Getting around the expense of cameras and equipment can be tough. One option is to buy used equipment. Sites such as eBay always have a ton of equipment for sale, but you have to trust the word of the seller about the condition of your purchase before you receive it. Large retailers such as KEH, B&H Photo, and Adorama also sell used equipment with ratings and various limited warranties. When buying a used camera body, bird photographer Paul Queneau recommends trying to learn how many "shutter cycles" (number of photos taken) the camera has been through, since camera shutters can and do wear out. For that reason, he's more comfortable buying used lenses than camera bodies.

It is also possible to rent camera equipment, either for specific outings or to see how you like certain brands and models. Online lens and camera companies offer rentals, or you might find something local. And, speaking of local, many brick-and-mortar camera shops have great sales around the holidays and again in the spring.

bounced around in the field, and the lenses did not have the sharpness that I craved for photographing birds.

What that means is that if you *really* want good bird shots, you might need to spend more money. A lot of money. How much more? Enough to permanently destroy your credit rating. As the title of this chapter indicates, you can easily blow a good part of your retirement savings (or if you're smart, your grandkids' college funds) on cameras, lenses, tripods, and other accessories. I've met photographers who spend well into the five digits *just on a camera lens*, though you don't have to spend quite that much for your first "somewhat serious" camera system.

Several camera companies make outstanding equipment. Different photographers swear by Sony, Nikon, Panasonic, OM Digital Systems (formerly Olympus), and Fujifilm. Personally, I have bought into the Canon photography universe, both because I started out with Canon and like their equipment, and because I find their cameras intuitive and easy to use. For the past four years, I have been using a Canon EOS 7D Mark II camera body (now discontinued, but similar to several other models) with an EF 100–400mm f/4.5–5.6L IS II USM zoom lens. This is a DSLR (digital single-lens reflex) camera, meaning that it has mirrors that reflect the image up to a viewfinder that you look through. When you press the shutter button, the main mirror snaps out of the way to allow the light to strike the camera's electronic sensor, capturing the photograph. A digital screen on the back of the camera allows you to immediately view the photo.

I have been pretty happy with this system. It's rugged, easy to use, and light enough for me to drag around without too much back strain. If there's good lighting and I am within twenty or thirty feet of most subjects, I can usually get publishable-quality photographs of birds with it. This system, though, is still a step below what most professional bird photographers use. More important, DSLR cameras are currently being swept away by a new generation of camera equipment.

### The Mirrorless Revolution

Most "serious" photographers that I know are switching from DSLR cameras to what are called "mirrorless" cameras. As their name suggests, mirrorless cameras don't rely on mirrors to bounce an image up to a viewfinder. Instead, the image lands directly on the camera's electronic sensor at all times. You still have a viewfinder, but it is electronic—like a TV screen—generated from the sensor. Phone cameras and point-and-shoot cameras are types of mirrorless cameras, but when people talk about mirrorless cameras these days, they are mainly talking about fancier cameras with interchangeable lenses.

One advantage to mirrorless cameras is that without the mirrors, the camera body can be smaller and lighter. However, for a bird photographer especially, other features provide superior performance over DSLR systems.

"I decided to go mirror-less about a year ago after previously shooting with a variety of DSLR setups," shares Uschi Carpenter, an accomplished nature photographer who captures some of the most stunning bird photographs I've ever seen. "Photographing with

a mirrorless camera has been a game changer in my bird photography. Two of the biggest advantages are (1) using the electronic shutter, which allows you to shoot in silent mode, and (2) the camera's capacity for eye detection, which will keep the focus on the eye while tracking a bird in flight."

This second feature has, frankly, got me drooling. As mentioned earlier, one of the keys to almost all wildlife photography is to have the animal's eye sharply focused—and this can be especially difficult with birds. Despite excellent autofocus capabilities, many cameras seem to get confused by feathers, and especially if a bird is moving around, it can be frustrating to try to capture a "sharp-eyed" bird. The latest, most advanced mirrorless cameras, however, offer incredible eye-tracking technology that can recognize an animal's eye and keep it in focus as you follow it.

Paul Queneau points out two other big advantages to mirrorless systems. One is that the latest high-end mirrorless bodies have a high-megapixel sensor that captures a larger digital image. "That really lets you crop in on a bird and still have a large print-quality photo," Queneau says. He also loves that on mirrorless systems you see the actual exposure of the photo before taking it. Especially for birds that are backlit against a bright sky, this allows you to quickly adjust your exposure before taking a picture.

Mirrorless technology is here to stay and will keep getting better. Meanwhile, many major brands have stopped developing any kind of new DSLR equipment, essentially leaving them as a "dead technology."

Bottom line: Mirrorless is something you'll want to consider before making a major purchase. If price is an obstacle, you might start with a beginning mirrorless camera and lens package. For a more advanced system, Queneau suggests looking at used mirrorless cameras and lenses (see the sidebar in this chapter, "Used Equipment and Renting").

## Postprocessing Software

Once you take the pictures, a second part of most people's photography workflow is to edit or process them using computer software. Carpenter, Queneau, and many other professional photographers use some version of Adobe Lightroom. For the beginning photographer, however, most camera manufacturers toss in free image processing software packages with their cameras. I find that Canon's Digital Photo Professional works just fine for many of the things I need to do. For Mac users, Apple Photos is free and "does a commendable job of simple edits and helping keep photos organized," says Queneau.

When it comes to processing, I pretty much just crop my photos, adjust the lighting, and occasionally, try to sharpen them. That doesn't mean that you can't do much more. I know one photographer who has become very successful using software to substitute exaggerated, psychedelic colors for the real colors in landscapes, sunsets, and other subjects.

Brave new world.

## Remember the Birds

No matter what level of photography expertise you aim for, remember that you have a responsibility to keep your subjects safe. Carpenter reminded me of one of the guiding principles of the National Audubon Society: *Place the welfare and safety of the birds and their habitats above all else and avoid disturbing them in any way.*

"All bird photographers want that perfect shot," she says, "and sometimes they'll go to great lengths to get it. The problem comes when that pursuit jeopardizes the welfare and safety of the birds themselves."

All of us birders have seen some overzealous photographer in the field trampling a bird's nesting area or scaring it away while trying to get a good photograph. If you ever have the impulse to do this—and believe me, you will—take a deep breath and remind yourself that it's not the end of the world if you *don't* get a great photo of this or that bird.

Another huge ethical photography concern is "owl baiting," which is the practice of some lazy photographers who lure owls and other raptors by setting out pet-store mice or other bait. This practice not only exposes the raptors to salmonella and other diseases but habituates them to humans, increasing their risk of getting struck by cars and other mishaps. An ethical concern for photographers and non-photographers alike is excessive use of playback (playing recordings of bird vocalizations) to attract birds. Braden and I occasionally use playback to draw out a bird, but try to do so only with common species and in situations where birds are not under stress from gazillions of other birders. Some photographers and other people, though, use this tool to the extreme, and to the possible detriment of their subjects. Do a search on the ABA Code of Birding Ethics for great guidance on this and similar topics.

As far as photography goes, Braden and I consider ourselves "opportunistic photographers" and I highly recommend this strategy for the vast majority of people. If a bird strikes the perfect pose right in front of us in good light and *demands* to be photographed, well, who are we to argue? More often than not, however, we will take what we can get without disturbing the bird and call it good. If you don't believe me, take a look at the many "just okay" shots on our blog!

For more on the ethics of wildlife photography, Carpenter recommends articles by eminent photographer and ethicist Melissa Groo, such as her post "Getting Closer" on the *Outdoor Photographer* website. Queneau recommends the online article "All About Owl Baiting" by Michael Furtman (see Resources).

## CHAPTER 25

# Big Years and Other Insane Ideas

As you develop more and more birding expertise—or perhaps even before then—it will be natural for you to start dreaming of different things you can do with your newfound skills and passion. We've already talked about local birding and traveling to different places, but for many birders their dreams manifest as a Big Year.

By now, you've probably gathered that a Big Year is an effort to see as many birds as possible within the ABA Area—or any other given area—in a calendar year. According to popular lore, the concept germinated when famed bird illustrator and writer Roger Tory Peterson decided to show his British pal James Fisher the American birds in 1953. During a hundred-day trip, documented in the book *Wild America*, the duo drove thirty thousand miles and even traveled to the Aleutian Islands in Alaska in search of birds, plants, and other wild species. Though a couple of people did record large annual bird counts prior to this, the concept of a Big Year didn't yet exist. Peterson and Fisher weren't trying to set a record, but they did anyway, seeing 572 different kinds of birds, and inspiring a trend.

Over the next sixteen years, their record was broken a couple of times while the ABA decided to standardize its official territory, also known as the ABA Area. This included the US (sans Hawai'i), Canada, the French territory of Saint Pierre and Miquelon (off the coast of Canada's New-foundland), and adjacent territorial waters. However, the idea of doing a Big Year didn't really take off until Kenn Kaufman and Floyd Murdoch both chased—and broke—the record in 1973 with 666 and 669 species respectively. Since then, other birders have broken, and sometimes obliterated, previous top totals. Before Hawai'i leaped into the ABA Area, John Weigel held the record with 784 species. After Hawai'i was added, John broke his own record, which now stands at 840—almost as many species as I have seen *in the entire world.*

All I can say is "Holy bird, Batman!"

Big Years are not without their detractors. Top Big Year birders spend obscene amounts of money and burn tons of fossil fuels driving and jetting back and forth across the country to see, say, a rare Whooper Swan in Washington or a La Sagra's Flycatcher in Florida, and it's no small irony that in pursuing birds they are also degrading the environment that birds depend on. Purists complain, too, that creating a competition out of birding detracts from the core of the hobby—learning about, enjoying, and protecting birds. Nonetheless, most birders pursuing a Big Year are not manically jet-setting to tick off species, and there is one inescapable fact about doing a Big Year: it can be a whole lot of fun!

## Our First Big Year

When it comes to Big Years, Braden and I usually do what we like to call Accidental or Opportunistic Big Years—those that have evolved primarily from business and other travel that we were going to do anyway. Only for our first Big Year did we plan some trips with the express purpose of birding. At that time, 2016, we had only a couple of years' experience under our belts, and it was mainly a desire to see and learn about species outside of Montana that compelled us to hit the road. We set a modest goal of seeing 250 species, but wondered if we would reach even that.

Our first out-of-state birding trip, to Arizona, confirmed that we'd set our sights too low, and we upped our goal to 300. After our second trip, to Texas, we raised it to 350. Those were the only two big trips

we had planned for the year, but after languishing for months at about 280 species, I whipped out the credit card and bought us tickets to California and the Monterey Bay Birding Festival, where we did a big all-day field trip to nab specialty birds such as Lawrence's Goldfinch and Yellow-billed Magpie. On that trip we also saw our first California Condors and took our first pelagic birding cruise, with famed trip leader Debi Shearwater, and yes, Braden did end up puking his guts out.

We ended up with 337 species for the year—short of our goal, but exceeding every other expectation. Our travels introduced Braden, then thirteen, to many incredible places he'd never been before. They also gave us irreplaceable father-son time together, and we met several new friends along the way. For both of us, though, the main benefit was that it doubled or tripled our knowledge of New World birds. After our Big Year, we felt like real birders for the first time and began approaching birding with vastly greater skills and perspective.

### Big Year Variants

I mention all of the above to demonstrate that doing a Big Year can serve as an incredibly fun, adventurous crash course in birds and birding. The best part is that you can decide what you want your Big Year to be and approach it in whatever way you want, and in whichever way accommodates your time and resources.

These are some of my favorite Big Year variations:
- Big Year by bicycle

- home state Big Year
- "patch" Big Year (species within a five-mile radius of your house)
- sparrow (or other bird group) Big Year
- county Big Year
- photographic Big Year (how many birds you can photograph)
- group Big Year (a group of birders sees how many species they can collectively find)

In 2020, Braden and I decided to do a Montana Big Year and got to know a lot more about our state. I ended up with 267 species that year while Braden tallied a whopping 275—not far short of our 2016 total for the entire ABA region! In 2022, Braden and I both "accidentally" smashed our personal ABA Big Year records when I recorded 374 species and Braden tallied a cool 500.

We may never again reach such numbers, but with birds, you never know.

## Other Fun Birding Goals and Challenges

Besides Big Years, birders have come up with flocks of other fun birding ideas. Many undertake Big Days, Big Weekends, and Big Months. In a hurry? Try speed birding! Say you're taking a long drive and you need to stretch—but not for too long. Pull over at a park or rest area, grab your binoculars, and see how many birds you can chase down in fifteen minutes.

A couple of summers ago, I began driving a truck for the US Forest Service here in Missoula. When fire equipment or supplies were needed at a wildfire in Montana or Idaho, they'd send me out in a pickup, one-ton, or five-ton delivery truck. It didn't take me long to challenge myself with a Truck Birding Big Year. I set a goal of seeing one hundred species while driving, and I got pretty close, tallying ninety-two species by the end of fire season.

Before the COVID pandemic, six-person birding teams could sign up for the annual Great American Arctic Birding Challenge, sponsored by Audubon Alaska. In this contest, teams from either Alaska or the Lower

48 worked to see how many Arctic breeding birds they could find between March 15 and June 1. What made it fun was that a team could be spread across the entire country! Braden and his friend Nick Ramsey did this a couple of times—and saw some great birds in the process. Hopefully, this challenge will resume soon.

Another fun team challenge I recently learned about is the Bird of the Day challenge (www.morgantingley.com/botd), created by UCLA professor Morgan Tingley. Each year, Tingley and his colleagues choose a bird for every day of the year. If you see that bird on that day, you earn a point. I haven't done this yet, but am seriously considering it.

## Christmas and Backyard Bird Counts

Several other birding activities deserve attention because of how they contribute to science and stoke birders' competitive natures.

The Christmas Bird Count (CBC; audubon.org/conservation/science /christmas-bird-count) is a venerable tradition first created as an alternative to a much more destructive tradition known, according to the Audubon website, as the Christmas "Side Hunt." In the Side Hunt, hunters would choose a location to see how many birds they could shoot in a day. "Why not count them instead?" proposed an ornithologist named James Chapman, and beginning in 1900, the Audubon Society organized an annual tradition that has grown and grown.

In recent years, more than a thousand CBCs have been conducted around the country, tallying almost twenty *million* birds annually. Each individual count takes place on a single day between December 14 and January 5, and undoubtedly one takes place near you. But why stop at one? Because local counts happen on different days, ambitious birders often participate in more than one CBC each year. Braden and I have gone on several and enjoyed them immensely. Not only do we learn new places to bird, we've also met some fantastic, friendly fellow birders and get to feel like we're contributing to a larger goal of monitoring winter bird populations.

The Great Backyard Bird Count (GBBC; birdcount.org) is a similar event and takes place over four days in February, starting the Friday before Presidents Day weekend. Individuals or teams stake out a place or places to bird. Then, they bird for at least fifteen minutes in each of those spots, reporting their results via eBird or Merlin. More than 384,000 people worldwide participated in one recent GBBC, recording an astounding 7,099 species of birds. Participation increases dramatically each year.

Project FeederWatch (feederwatch.org) enlists citizen scientists across the US and Canada to record birds at static locations from November through April. This data helps scientists amass detailed information about the winter abundance and distributions of hundreds of species, as well as the timing of their movements.

Every May 14, eBird sponsors an annual Global Big Day event (ebird .org/globalbigday) in which more than fifty thousand birders around the globe head out to tally all the birds they can find on a single day. These birders generally find *even more* birds than GBBC birders—almost 7,800 species in one recent year—and here, friendly competition between countries rears its head. Even though it has one-tenth the birders as the United States, Colombia generally trounces the competition with more than 1,550 species. That's more than twice the number tallied in the US! In that same year, Peru, Ecuador, Brazil, India, Bolivia, and Mexico followed, leaving the US in a dismal eighth place. It's all in good fun, however, and best of all, birders are gathering vital information for scientists and the conservation community.

All of this should make you realize that the only limit to making birding fun is your imagination—and the birds, of course. Whether you are doing some kind of Big Year, patch birding around your neighborhood, or participating in the Christmas Bird Count or Global Big Day, just remember to enjoy and appreciate the remarkable creatures in front of you.

## CHAPTER 26

# Bringing Friends and Family into the Flock

One potential pitfall of fully embracing birds is that not all of your friends and family will understand your new obsession. Some will ask why you need to go birding when you could be playing golf, taking a cooking class, or sleeping in until noon. Some might even complain that birding doesn't leave enough time for you to spend with *them*. When this happens, do not for a moment doubt the correctness of your new passion. Others, well, they simply have not yet achieved avian enlightenment, or what the ancients simply called Bhirdism.

What to do? Well, the first thing, of course, is to reassure the people you love that you still love them, and that your enthusiasm for birds in no way lessens your desire to maintain a close relationship with them. Demonstrate your devotion by occasionally going bowling with them, play-

ing board games, going out to dinner—whatever they enjoy doing in your company. At the same time, start experimenting with ways to involve your loved ones at least peripherally in your new hobby. In Bhirdism, we call this "showing them the nest." How? Here are a few solid—and one or two questionable—suggestions.

### Set Up a Backyard Bird Feeder or Bath

Even people with little interest in animals often get sucked in by seeing actual, real wildlife, so take advantage of the suggestions way back in Chapter 8: Feeders, Houses, and Water Features: A Great Way to Begin, and create more opportunities for birds to make an appearance. With a little help and education from you ("Hey, look at that Blue-footed Booby diving into the fountain!"), others may subconsciously develop an interest. This works especially well if you have colorful local birds such as cardinals, goldfinches, and jays. As your friends and loved ones see the avian wonders visiting your yard, they will ask you questions about what they are seeing. Eventually, some of these folks may accept your invitations to go birding—and that's when you've got 'em hooked!

### Plan Vacations Full of Flamboyant Birds

Very few people are immune to the sight of dozens of shockingly colorful parrots, toucans, tanagers, and other birds swirling around them. And sure, you *can* find curious and colorful birds in places such as Miami and Bakersfield, California, where introduced parrots have taken hold, but a much better bet is to, if it is within your means, plan a family trip to Mexico, Hawai'i, Australia, or the Amazon. Especially if you include a couple of nature walks or a boat trip, the magnificence of birds will be hard for your loved ones to ignore, and they may return home imbued with their own Born Again birding passions.

### Buy Everyone Bird Calendars

Can't swing a full-on vacation? A much more affordable option is to buy bird calendars for your friends and family. I love bird calendars. Several times a week I find myself studying one, quizzing myself on the birds and asking questions about them. It's a great way to get others interested too. Especially if you choose calendars with photos of multiple species for each month, friends and family members may idly begin perusing the different birds and checking out what they are. With luck, this will set off a domino effect and before you know it, they will beg to come birding with you.

## Start a Business That Earns Billions by Promoting Birds

Expanding on the previous suggestion, imagine that *you* are the one making and selling bird calendars, T-shirts, mugs, or other bird-related items. This is the best possible situation, because if your family's economic livelihood depends on birds, they will have to get on board. "What? You want to go to *college*? Start pasting on shipping labels, Junior. Oh, so you're tired of the car breaking down? Get out on that street corner and schlep some shirts!" Sure, they may resent such a heavy-handed approach, but what can they do? You've got them right where you want them, and they will have no choice but to fully embrace birds and birding. If you do it right, you will make enough money to easily afford family therapy sessions later.

UNFORTUNATELY, IT'S POSSIBLE that none of the above suggestions will work. I mean, let's face it, if your significant other isn't into birds after a year or two, they may not ever come around. However, that doesn't mean you can't strike a good compromise. Even though she's not a birder, my wife doesn't mind going out on a birding adventure now and then, and even appreciates the chance to get outside. When we vacation, I like to get up early while she enjoys sleeping in. Guess what I do in the morning? Strap on my binoculars and camera and get in a few hours birding before breakfast.

Other couples reach their own accommodations. Braden and I run into one birding couple all over Montana. The woman is an avid birder and has even attempted to set some state Big Year records. The man? Well, he is so-so about birds, but he does like to drive his wife around to different refuges and hotspots, so it's a good mutualistic relationship.

It's especially important, and I say this with all seriousness, to get people involved when they are young. It doesn't work with every kid, but if you invest time taking your children or grandchildren birding—teaching them how to use binoculars and showing them some cool birds—your chance of creating a "bird convert" is much greater than if you wait until someone is, well, our age. Almost all young people have an innate appreciation for animals, and they equally appreciate that you are willing to spend time talking to them, listening to them, and showing them things. Buy them an ice cream afterward. Make it fun. They will love you for it, and you might just find yourself with a new birding companion.

If you fail to find a true birding companion within the circle of your family and friends, take heart. You will undoubtedly find one—or perhaps a dozen—as you get out there birding in the field. Even if your family members don't share your birding passions, they usually will appreciate that you have something that continues to light your fire as you enter your later decades. The fact that you are continuing to learn and have adventures in life often has a trickle-down effect, inspiring your loved ones to pursue their own passions and interests. Taking time to be supportive of them in what they love will likely earn that same respect and support when it's your time to bird.

# PART VII

# GIVING BACK TO BIRDS

*We believe that birders with passion can change the world for the better. . . . And that those birders who are crazy enough to think they can change the world are the ones who actually do.*
—Steve Jobs

## CHAPTER 27

# Birds in Peril:
# The Big Picture

An inescapable feature of living in the times that we do is that many of the things we loved and cherished during our lifetimes are in danger of vanishing forever. That, unfortunately, includes many of Earth's bird species. As a person who loves and enjoys birds, I consider it a moral obligation to stay reasonably well informed about the state of the world's birds, and even more important, to do what I can to help protect them. I hope that you will, too, because birds need our help like never before.

Every couple of years a little-known group with a really long name releases a report that summarizes the overall state of birds in North America, or addresses specific aspects of bird conservation based on trends or policies. This group, the NABCI—or North American Bird Conservation Initiative—is made up of representatives from an astonishing array of heavy hitters including government agencies, private conservation organizations, and academic institutions from the United States, Canada, and Mexico. It includes the US Fish and Wildlife Service, the US Department of Agriculture, Ducks Unlimited, the National Audubon Society, the American Bird Conservancy, and almost anyone else you can think of involved in bird conservation.

When the US arm of the NABCI released its most recent *State of the Birds, United States of America* (see Sources), it was a sobering document.

According to the report, one in four breeding birds—three billion individuals—had been lost in the US and Canada over the past fifty years. At first you might think, "Hm. Only one-quarter of the birds? That's not so bad, is it?" But this has been within the very short lifetimes of most of you reading this—not even a flick of a proverbial tail feather. If you were watching some sort of

time-lapse video of bird populations over the past several thousand years and you reached the last fifty, it would look like an atomic bomb had gone off *right now*.

And it gets worse. The report identified seventy "tipping point" birds that had lost two-thirds of their populations in the last fifty years, and are anticipated to lose *another* 50 percent in just the next fifty years. These are not all esoteric, little-known species. They include many well-known birds that you and I may have grown up with such as the Bobolink, Chimney Swift, Evening Grosbeak, Pinyon Jay, Ruddy Turnstone, Short-billed Dowitcher, and Whimbrel.

The report emphasized that birds had declined in every major habitat type except one—wetlands, which showed a population increase because of widespread conservation efforts. More on that later. Below are the numbers for other habitats.

- Western Forest Birds............................................−5 percent
- Aridland Birds.....................................................−26 percent
- Eastern Forest Birds...........................................−27 percent

- Sea Ducks..............................................................−30 percent
- Shorebirds..........................................................−33 percent
- Grassland Birds.................................................−34 percent

Now, birds are notoriously difficult to count, and you can quibble about the numbers, but the trends are clear: many of our birds are experiencing catastrophic declines.

Beyond North America, the numbers aren't any better. One of Braden's and my favorite conservation groups is BirdLife International. In fact, I'll wait while you send them a big donation right now . . .

. . .

(humming)

. . .

Okay, all finished? Great! Earth's birds thank you! Anyway, BirdLife International supports bird conservation projects the world over and is involved in extensive monitoring of birds and their habitats. In their annual *State of the World's Birds*, BirdLife's CEO Patricia Zurita neatly encapsulated what's going on worldwide:

*Nature is in decline across the world, with unsustainable development degrading natural habitats and driving species to extinction. Threats such as agricultural expansion and intensification, logging, invasive alien species and overexploitation continue to drive this trend, while climate change is not only a threat in itself, but also exacerbates many existing pressures.*

ONE OF BIRDLIFE INTERNATIONAL'S activities is to serve as the scientific bird authority for the International Union for the Conservation of Nature. The IUCN's Red List seeks to document the status of every animal and plant species on the planet, assigning each a category, or ranking, based on how threatened or endangered it is. It's a massive job, and taxonomic groups such as mammals, amphibians, reptiles, and fish have not been fully evaluated. Thanks to the world's intense interest in birds, however, the majority of bird species has been studied and given a ranking.

Data from the Red List indicate that 49 percent of the world's roughly 11,000 bird species are declining, while only 38 percent are stable and 6 percent increasing. Another 6 percent could not be evaluated. That doesn't mean that half of the world's bird species are endangered—not yet. Many of them are, however. According to the report, about one-fifth of bird species are either threatened or likely to become threatened soon. This includes 231 species that are critically endangered.

I could keep throwing numbers at you for many more pages, but you get the picture: Human beings are clearly not managing the planet in a way that bodes well for the future, and birds are a major indicator of what's going on. The two documents I cited above, along with literally thousands of other scientific studies and reports, demonstrate that species numbers plummet as their habitats degrade and disappear. That's a problem for a lot of reasons. Besides offering people unparalleled enjoyment and intellectual interest, birds perform myriad ecological services such as pest control, pollination, seed dispersal, and nutrient recycling. These services, worth billions—perhaps trillions—of dollars to humans, are being lost as bird numbers decline.

But here's the thing: Most of our species are eminently savable. I mentioned before that wetland birds had actually shown population increases in the past fifty years. It's no coincidence that funding for waterfowl conservation has been massive, both from private and public sources. Groups such as Ducks Unlimited, Audubon, and the US Fish and Wildlife Service have poured hundreds of millions of dollars into creating and protecting wetlands, educating hunters and other wetlands users, and monitoring populations. This work has paid off, especially for ducks, geese, and swans. Numbers for dabbling and diving ducks alone increased a healthy 34 percent during the same time period other groups of birds have been declining.

To sum it all up, the world is in trouble, and that means birds are in trouble. As birders, we have a choice. Do we sit back and watch it happen, or do we get involved and try to turn things around? For me, the answer is obvious. Birders can not only make a great difference as individuals, but we hold enormous power to influence policy, promote conservation, and elect politicians who truly understand and are willing to act.

From personal experience, I can tell you that while helping birds is fun, it also makes me feel a hell of a lot better about the world. The next few chapters offer specific suggestions on how to help birds—and on how to shape our own birding activities to have minimal impacts on the animals we love.

## CHAPTER 28

# Helping Birds: The Basics

Despite the alarming news about the state of the world's birds, there are many things we can do to improve the situation. Birds as a whole tend to be resilient creatures, and given half a chance, they bounce back. Think about the incredible rebound of raptors following the banning of the pesticide DDT in the early 1970s—or the reappearance of the California Condor in the West following dedicated conservation efforts. Protecting the many other threatened species is a mammoth task and will take much wider awareness and actions. Let's start with the basics.

## Support Bird Conservation Groups

I have already touched on this in several places in the book, but giving to conservation groups is one of the most valuable things you can do to support birds. A person's ability to do this varies, of course, but is almost always greater than we think.

Below are groups that make significant differences in protecting birds and their habitats. Besides working to protect birds directly, most of these groups also focus on climate change, urban sprawl, clean energy, and other larger issues that have direct impacts on birds and our planet. Most recognize the links between conservation and social justice, and they work closely with local and Indigenous communities to create plans that help both birds and people. Since laws and public policy are critical to protecting birds, they are involved in those arenas too. My family and I donate to almost all of these groups, and we take satisfaction in knowing that every buck we part with is an investment both in birds and in our collective future. If you're not able to or comfortable giving money, volunteering is another great way to pitch in.

- American Bird Conservancy abcbirds.org
- American Birding Association aba.org
- BirdLife International birdlife.org
- Center for Biological Diversity biologicaldiversity.org
- Conservation International conservation.org
- Cornell Lab of Ornithology birds.cornell.edu/home
- Ducks Unlimited ducks.org
- National Audubon Society Regional, state, and local Audubon chapters audubon.org
- The Peregrine Fund peregrinefund.org
- Union of Concerned Scientists ucsusa.org

## Reduce Your Energy Consumption

Climate change may be the greatest challenge for birds and people going forward. Increasing temperatures are already roasting many parts of the planet, and they likely play a major role in generating more severe droughts, hurricanes, and other extreme weather events. As temperatures rise, they also are eliminating vital habitats for many birds. Many, perhaps most, birds are already shifting their ranges to accommodate changing temperatures, but birds such as White-tailed Ptarmigans and Brown-capped Rosy-Finches will literally have no place to go when the last high-altitude breeding habitat with year-round snow disappears.

To combat rising temperatures, the simplest thing each of us can do is reduce how much energy we use. Most electricity is still produced by burning fossil fuels, and so each time we turn off a light, we are giving the planet a little break. Even in places where solar and wind power are becoming more common, it takes fossil fuels to *create* these facilities. The less electricity we use, the fewer windmills and solar panels have to be installed, again helping out the planet.

Of course we also consume large amounts of fossil fuels directly when we drive cars and heat our houses. Ask yourself, "Do I really need to run to the store for my frosted brown-sugar cinnamon Pop-Tarts *right now*, or can I wait till tomorrow when I'm on my way to work?" Or, in winter, "Would my life really be so bad if I turned down the thermostat two degrees and put on a sweater?"

I think about such things a lot because I fly more than the average person. How do I come to terms with this? Well, like most people, I compromise. In my own case, I almost always combine birding with travel I am going to do anyway, either for work or to visit family. And although I fly more than most people, I drive a lot less, reducing the planet's $CO_2$ burden as much as possible. With the help of federal tax credits, my family and I decided to take a further step last year and invest in rooftop solar panels to generate our own clean energy.

I could provide plenty of other examples for how to reduce our carbon footprints, both big and small, but let's face it, we all pretty much know how to reduce our energy consumption. As a society, though, we've gotten lazy about it. Do you remember all the great public service ads from the sixties and seventies about quitting smoking, wearing seatbelts, recycling, and turning off lights? What happened to those? We need to bring them back—with energy conservation being top of the list!

## Prevent Window Strikes

As with most large-scale wildlife questions, it's difficult to pin down how many birds die from striking buildings, but a 2014 study by Smithsonian researchers put the estimate at between 365 million and 1 billion birds annually, so collisions with buildings present a major problem.

Strikes are highest during spring and fall migration, when birds are attracted to lights left on in buildings at night. Recently, nearly a thousand migrating birds died *in a single night* after colliding with Chicago's McCormick Place building complex. A number of groups are attempting

to tackle this issue by asking businesses, governments, and individuals to turn off their lights during migration seasons—and take measures to make windows less reflective. This makes sense both economically and for birds, so it seems like a win-win for everyone.

Not all bird strikes happen at night, however. From the outside, many windows act like mirrors and look like open space or sky to birds. We had at least two birds hit the windows of our current house before Braden devised a simple solution. He cut out paper outlines of birds and affixed them to our largest plate-glass windows to show birds that something was there to avoid. I have to say they make me smile every time I see them, and even better, we haven't had a bird strike since. If you don't want to make cutouts for yourself, there are quite a few attractive commercial decals for sale. These are more effective if mounted on the outside of the windows. External window screens also reduce collisions, and more sophisticated bird-friendly-glass solutions are available for people constructing new or retrofitting existing buildings.

I had always assumed that most impacts occurred on tall buildings, but this isn't true, at least partly because there are so many more low- and medium-height buildings than skyscrapers. The vast majority of birds are killed colliding with lower buildings, so even if you have a single-level home, you can help by turning off your lights at night and taking the above-mentioned steps to reduce bird strikes during daylight hours.

## CHAPTER 29

# The Bird-Friendly Yard

When we moved into our house eighteen years ago, I knew I wanted to fill the yard with native plants to the greatest extent possible. I was fed up with the typical combo of useless lawn and even more useless exotic landscape plants that most Americans think is attractive, thanks to the efforts of lazy landscapers. I had not yet embraced birding, but still felt bent on creating something that would serve as habitat for native birds, insects, and other animals. I even had some experience in this regard, having put in a native garden at our previous place with terrific results. Native coneflower, bee balm, and liatris bloomed gloriously each spring, nourishing a host of butterfly and other insect species, and I imagined recreating the same thing on a grander scale at our new place.

The deer loved me for it.

I planted dozens of native flowers, shrubs, and trees, and then watched as the deer tore them out one by one. They didn't *eat* all of them, mind you. They just gave many of them a sniff and ripped them out by the roots. They especially loved the so-called deer-resistant plants that I put in, taking great delight in chowing them down and then laughing at me as I fumed a few yards away. After several weeks of this, I began studying venison recipes, but I also kept trying to build the yard of my dreams. I never did achieve the glory of our old place, but eventually enough plants survived to create a fairly nice habitat for birds and insects.

# Nature's Best Hope

Turning yards into habitat is nothing new, but the concept has been widely promoted by author Douglas W. Tallamy, especially in his popular book *Nature's Best Hope: A New Approach to Conservation That Starts in Your Yard*. According to Tallamy, 40 million acres in the United States—an area the size of New England—have been converted from productive natural ecosystems into, you guessed it, lawns. "A 2005 turfgrass study," Tallamy writes, "showed that the small state of Maryland alone had 1.1 million acres of lawn—more than twice the area allocated to its state parks, state forests, and wildlife management areas combined."

With the vast majority of our nation's land under private ownership, Tallamy explains that people like you and me have an incredible opportunity to turn this unproductive acreage into a game-changing conservation revolution by planting native plants over exotics. He cites scientific studies demonstrating the vastly superior role of native plants in supporting the insects that create thriving, functioning ecosystems. Returning our lawns to productive ecosystems would not only attract birds and other wildlife, he argues, but would help restore the interconnectedness of habitats critical to the survival of plants and animals.

Tallamy calls his plan the Homegrown National Park, because if Americans collectively converted only *half* of our lawn space to functioning habitat, it would be larger than Everglades, Yellowstone, Yosemite, Grand Teton, Canyonlands, Mount Rainier, North Cascades, Badlands, Olympic, Sequoia, Grand Canyon, Denali, and Great Smoky Mountains National Parks combined.

Tallamy's books are required reading for birders, and will irrevocably transform how you look at that sterile expanse of green grass that might lie outside your window.

I recount this story partly because I still bitterly resent the duplicity of our neighborhood deer, but also to encourage you in your own landscape ambitions. If you have *any* kind of yard, one of the most rewarding things you can do is grow plants that are useful to wildlife, including birds. In fact, I prefer doing this to putting out bird feeders. Feeders are fine, but what if you can't fill them for some reason, or forget? What if someone buys your house who, heaven forbid, doesn't care about bird feeders? In these cases, the plants (hopefully) will still be there, offering reliable resources to birds and other wildlife year after year.

## What to Plant?

So what kinds of plants should you put in your new bird-friendly yard? When I first started researching native flora, I thought that berry and other obvious food plants would be the most important to the birds, and many species do take advantage of our plants that produce berries, nectar, and to a lesser extent, seeds. What the birds also require, however, are native shrubs that provide cover and insects. Our favorite backyard visitors—chickadees, nuthatches, and seasonally, kinglets, wrens, and warblers—are mostly bug hunters who flit around inside bushes, where they are presumably safer from predators. Our yard also serves as a nesting location for a hardy pair of Song Sparrows in some years, while flickers and juncos drop by to root around for ants and seeds on the ground under the feeder.

With all this in mind, I suggest that if you are creating a bird-friendly habitat in your yard, select a nice variety of food and shelter plants appropriate to your climate zone. At our house in Montana, we've had excellent success with buffaloberry, golden currant, aspen, ocean spray, and bur oak. One of the coolest things on Audubon's website is the Native Plants Database (audubon.org/native-plants) where you can look up which plants to install based on your location and what you want to attract to your yard. The National Wildlife Federation has a similar site called Garden for Wildlife (gardenforwildlife.com). If you lack a local native plant nursery, both organizations will even sell you the plants you want and have them delivered to your door. How great is that?

Many gardeners point out that native plants are not the only plants that offer valuable resources to birds. A number of exotic flowers and bushes produce nectar, seeds, and fruits that birds love. As writers such as Douglas Tallamy explain, however, first appearances can be deceiving. Many seemingly "birdy" introduced plants do not support a fraction of the quantity or diversity of insects that native plants do, and the berries of many introduced plants fail to provide the fat content that migrating species especially need. Before choosing any exotics, do your due diligence and make sure none of your choices are likely to become invasive where you live.

## Lessons Learned and Other Strategies

Here are a few more thoughts from my own experiences that may save you trouble and prove highly entertaining:

- Unless you really know what you're doing, never plant grasses of any kind. It's true that some grasses behave and stick to their own allotted ground, but in my experience most spread and become nuisances in no time.

- If you have a dead tree with a diameter of at least twelve inches, and it's not about to flatten your car or crush your grandkids' portable swimming pool, consider leaving it standing. Woodpeckers rely on dead trees to drill out nesting and

# A Yard Grows in Brooklyn

Don't have a big yard? Never fear. You can create important bird habitat in the tiniest of spaces. Even planting a single bird-friendly bush can provide food and shelter to native birds.

Consider the "yard" of veteran children's book editor Harold Underdown. He and his family live in a brownstone in Brooklyn, New York, with about seven or eight hundred square feet of bare ground behind it. When they moved in, the space was full of weeds and construction debris, and a thin layer of dirt covered two concrete paths leading down both sides of it. Undeterred, he and his wife and daughter set about transforming their tiny bit of "acreage."

"Initially we just wanted to have attractive plants to look at," Underdown explains. "We brought some with us from our previous place, and our first plantings included clematis, some balloon flowers, a butterfly bush, columbine, echinacea, and foxgloves—which did not do well and are now gone. More recently we've planted native honeysuckle, some tall species of lilies, and a few rose bushes. We also have plants in pots on the patio."

Though Underdown's efforts didn't initially focus on wildlife, the animals were apparently unaware of this. Over the years, more than twenty species of birds have shown up, including some "big city surprises" such as titmice, juncos, cardinals, jays, juncos, and most recently, a Red-bellied Woodpecker. Their biggest shocker? A Cooper's Hawk in the dead of winter.

The birds have been joined by monarch and swallowtail butterflies, spiders, an assortment of bugs—even fireflies in summer. The abundance of wildlife has, in turn, made Underdown focus more on what animals need. "We plan to do more planting of native plants that produce berries or seeds the birds want. That's the next phase!" Underdown also points out that their simple bird bath has been a huge success. "The birds drink from it, bathe in it . . . It's lots of fun."

roosting cavities—and other cavity-nesting birds rely on woodpeckers to do this. If the tree is really tall and you need to remove it for safety reasons, consider leaving at least fifteen or twenty feet of the trunk. As always, use common sense and safety in making your decision.

- If deer are a problem for you, as they are for me, fence off some areas that deer can't reach. Thanks to our dog, Lola, deer don't leap over our four-foot fence into the backyard, leaving this as a great place to plant all kinds of things. Out in front, we've enclosed several areas for our "deer-resistant" (har har) flowers. Note that the height of a deer fence is generally between six and ten feet, but deer usually avoid jumping into small, narrow enclosures, so you can often get away with something shorter for these.

- Invasive House Sparrows can be a huge nuisance for people wanting to attract native birds. They repeatedly tried to take over my backyard feeders, and for several years, they brutally bullied the chickadees who were trying to nest in our birdhouses. Finally, I bought a sparrow trap (sparrowtraps.net), which has been very effective. And yes, I *do* kill the House Sparrows after I catch them, since releasing them somewhere else just moves the problem to another location. Not everyone has the stomach for this, but I look at these invasive birds the same way I do at rats, cockroaches, and other pests. If you decide to try this, it's imperative to monitor the trap every few hours to make sure you haven't caught a Song Sparrow, junco, or other native bird.

## CHAPTER 30

# Keeping Cats Indoors

I had planned to include a discussion of cats in the previous chapter, but cats arouse such strong passions among birders and play such a large role in the destruction of wildlife that I decided to devote an entire chapter to them.

To begin, let's acknowledge that pet cats offer millions of people irreplaceable companionship and amusement, and are often considered an essential part of the family. It's no surprise, then, that when I start describing cats as implacable killers who are contributing to the rapid annihilation of wildlife around the globe—well, it's going to generate strong reactions.

Unfortunately, outdoor cats have earned this notorious reputation.

The American Bird Conservancy identifies outdoor cats as the number-one human-generated threat to birds in the United States and Canada. Almost everywhere Braden and I bird, we've seen outdoor cats hunting, often lying in wait near feeding or nesting birds. Many people still shrug this off as something natural, with cats just following their instincts as part of the cycle of life. And that might be true—if we lived in the Middle East. According to the latest thought, this is where domestic cats evolved from similar wild ancestors, so we might assume that Middle Eastern birds have at least some adaptations to this type of predator.

However, in North and South America, Australia, New Zealand, and many other parts of the world, cats have proven to be an immensely

destructive invasive species. Why? Because these are places where many native animals evolved without any exposure to a housecat-like predator. Here in the US we have no other common, native, mid-size predator that is great at both stalking and at lying in wait for prey. As a result, many of our bird, mammal, reptile, and amphibian species evolved to be totally unequipped to deal with this threat and have suffered accordingly.

## Cat-Tastrophes

In the United States alone, estimates of the number of outdoor cats—both feral and pets—range between about 30 and 100 million, and a scientific paper that came out in 2013 put their toll on birds at *between 1.3 and 4 billion per year*. It's worth saying a few words about this study, titled "The Impact of Free-Ranging Domestic Cats on Wildlife of the United States," because as its authors acknowledge, very little research has been done on just how many birds cats are killing. Many people, in fact, view this paper's estimate with skepticism and, I think, rightly so. That shouldn't keep us from seeing the forest for the trees, however.

A little scratch-pad math shows that it wouldn't take much for this estimate to be correct. Thirty million outdoor cats (the lower end of estimates) would each have to kill only about thirty-three birds per year to bring the toll to one billion birds. One hundred million outdoor cats would each need to kill only ten birds a year—something that seems entirely plausible given that most outdoor cats are hunting every single day. But even if the number of birds being killed is *one-tenth* of that estimate—one hundred million birds per year—that's still a hell of a lot of birds.

In a more recent study titled "The Small Home Ranges and Large Local Ecological Impacts of Pet Cats," researchers collared and tracked almost nine hundred domestic cats in the US, United Kingdom, Australia, and New Zealand—with similarly dramatic results. On average, each cat brought home forty-two "kills" during the year, but since cats don't always share their kills with their owners, the researchers estimated the actual toll was closer to triple that number. And this was for well-fed domestic outdoor cats. Researchers believe that feral cats have a much greater impact on wildlife.

Wherever you live, when you start birding you will no doubt make your own observations about the toll of outdoor cats on birds. Braden and I spot outdoor cats on farms and ranches but also in nature areas, wildlife refuges, urban parks, and neighborhoods. Some of our most disturbing experiences have been in city parks in places from Miami to Merced, California, and especially Latin America. In many of these, feral cats—along with invasive iguanas, squirrels, and other animals—roamed everywhere, with hardly a bird to be seen. Based on location and time of year, these places should have been teeming with birds, but instead they were eerily quiet, occupied mainly by mangy, half-starved kitties.

Scientists believe that Dark-eyed Juncos, flickers, rails, and other ground birds have been especially hard-hit, but cats can and will take any sort of bird they can reach. Not long ago Braden and I chased away a very plump cat stalking Black-throated Blue Warblers in Brooklyn's Pioneer

Park. It wouldn't be so bad if humans could train cats to hunt only other invasive species such as House Sparrows and European Starlings, but alas, those species *did* evolve with cats and seem adept at avoiding them. For all our other species, it's time to start seeing outdoor cats for the unnatural menace that they are.

## The TNRM Fantasy

Around the country, certain animal welfare groups have proposed a solution to feral cats called Trap, Neuter, Release (TNR), or alternatively, Trap, Neuter, Release, Monitor (TNRM). The idea is to catch outdoor cats, get them "fixed," and then return them to the outdoors to live out the rest of their natural lives, sometimes while being fed, supposedly to reduce their predatory instincts. Since these cats can no longer reproduce, the thinking is that their populations will slowly decrease until they disappear.

Unfortunately, TNRM programs take *enormous* amounts of money, time, and dedication and have been attempted in only a handful of locations. Studies on their effectiveness have been mixed, but what's clear is that TNRM does not solve the problem of feral cats—and may even be making it worse. Cats that are returned to the outdoors continue to roam the landscape, killing more and more wildlife. Cat colonies often don't shrink, but instead attract more cats and become dumping grounds for unwanted cats, requiring that the colonies be maintained by people indefinitely.

Releasing cats back into the wild also isn't doing them any favors. The lifetime of an average feral cat is extremely short; the consensus seems to be around two years. These cats get run over by cars, or are ravaged by disease, coyotes, and in our neighborhood, territorial raccoons. I was surprised to learn that even the animal rights group PETA (People for the Ethical Treatment of Animals) opposes TNR as inhumane and ineffective. According to their spokesperson, "The bottom line is that TNR makes *humans*—not cats and certainly not wildlife—feel better."

If we truly want to save our wildlife for future generations, we need to view cats as we do other invasive pests and institute vigorous humane—

and yes, when called for, lethal—control programs that give native birds, mammals, reptiles, and other species a chance. Several councils in Australia have banned outdoor cats, and the entire country is moving closer to a nationwide "outdoor cat crackdown," increasing the prospects that its unique wildlife will survive into the next century. It's time for Americans to wake up and also see the threat, and we birders can serve as powerful education ambassadors in making this happen.

Meanwhile, if you have a cat, you can immediately make a huge difference to birds simply by keeping Kitty inside. Colorful collars or "kitty bells" don't suffice to warn birds—and do not prevent cats from killing them. Only keeping the cat inside guarantees that it will not kill wildlife. Kitty may complain a bit, and you will no doubt have to clean out the litter box more frequently, but you'll have the satisfaction that you are making a solid, *real* contribution to saving our wildlife for the next generation.

## CHAPTER 31

# Leading Bird Trips and Teaching Classes

Raise your hand if you read this chapter title and thought "Oh, come on!" or "Me? Yeah, right!" Honestly, I would have thought the same thing when I began birding less than a decade ago, but here's the thing: if you start birding on a regular basis, you will be astonished by how quickly you build knowledge. Even a person who has been birding only a couple of years is an absolute expert compared to novices—and that provides you with abundant opportunities to teach others about birds and their importance to our planet.

My first experience teaching about birds happened almost entirely by accident. It was 2018 and my memoir *Warblers & Woodpeckers: A Father-Son Big Year of Birding* had just been published. Trying to think ahead, I reached out to the director of one prominent birding festival and asked if she might be interested in having me speak at the festival in 2020. She liked the idea and we agreed to keep in touch about it.

A few months later, I got a surprise call from her. She had booked Bill Thompson III, legendary author and then publisher of *Bird Watcher's Digest*, as one of her star speakers for the 2019 conference. Unfortunately, she explained, Thompson had been forced to cancel because of illness. Could Braden and I fill in? "Are you kidding me?" I almost shouted. In addition to having me give a talk, the director asked if we would help lead two Big Day birding outings with festival participants. Braden and I thought twice, unsure if we really knew enough about birds to take that on, but we also realized we might never get a similar opportunity again and eagerly accepted.

The first trip did not go well. The main leader had been birding for several centuries and had become, well, a grump. He was hell-bent on hitting every place on his itinerary and racking up the highest bird total possible. I don't blame him for that, except it was obvious that most of the participants didn't really care about such things and wanted to spend more time enjoying the birds right in front of them. He bawled out several of the birders—and me—for lollygagging, and it kind of soured the day.

The second trip couldn't have gone more differently. It was led by a fabulously enthusiastic local birder who pushed hard but also went with the flow, and we all had an amazing time. Braden impressed everyone with his bird knowledge, and I was able to keep up and help others most of the time. We also scored an impressive 130+ species for the day—still a one-day record for us.

In a sad footnote, Bill Thompson III died shortly after that festival, leaving a giant hole in the birding world. As up and down as our two field trips turned out, though, they showed both Braden and me that we had learned enough about birds to teach others. Since those first field trips, I have been asked to lead trips at several other festivals, and they have all been great experiences. I also have given dozens of lectures to people about different kinds of birds—but there's more.

As a children's book author, I'm often invited to visit schools, mainly to talk about writing and reading and science. These days, I am *also* asked to lead birding field trips for some of the students, and I tell you, it's a blast. Having twenty youngsters with binoculars all calling out animals while falling in puddles, losing their jackets, and asking to go to the bathroom is an experience I can only compare to getting caught in a Category F2 or F3 tornado. In our screen-dominated society, though, having the chance to get a group of kids out into nature is something none of us should pass up. Even when you think the kids aren't paying attention to the birds, many of them are, and I have little doubt most of them will remember the experience.

## Creative Teaching

As the above examples demonstrate, opportunities to share your knowledge are all around you, and the world needs your knowledge, compassion, and experience. Wherever your journey has taken you in the last forty, fifty, sixty years or more, you are endowed with a unique set of skills and connections that can benefit others, and teaching about birds is an instant way to make the world a better place.

Have you ever thought of becoming a merit badge counselor? I served as an assistant scoutmaster for my son's Boy Scout troop, and signed up to be a counselor for about a dozen wildlife-, science-, and literacy-related merit badges, including bird study. Scouting troops and similar youth groups are hungry for counselors these days, and even though Braden finished up his scouting career long ago, I continued to serve as one for several years—something you can do whether or not you have kids or grandkids in such programs.

Many local colleges and adult ed programs accept proposals from people to teach new courses, and birding classes are always popular. Once you have a few years of birding under your belt, believe me, you will be qualified to teach one. And just to be clear, you do *not* need to know every single bird you see or hear to teach one of these classes. One of the wonderful things about birding with others is that it's a collaborative experience. While leading a birding trip at the HummerBird Celebration in Rockport, Texas, I stopped our group to look at a hawk in the distance. I didn't know what it was, and neither did the local expert, but we and the other birders studied it and looked at our guides, and together we finally concluded it was a Broad-winged Hawk—a lifer for me. This kind of thing happens frequently out in the field and is part of what makes birding so fun, even if you are leading the trip.

Of course not all of your endeavors will succeed. I tried to start a birding club at my daughter's high school and could never get a critical mass of kids interested. Even so, I like to think that I kindled a love of nature in one or two young people. You just have to take such failures in stride, learn from them, and apply them to your next opportunity, whatever that may be.

## CHAPTER 32

# Birding Politics

Not long ago, I read an article on the efficacy of spending money in different ways to help the environment. The upshot was this: Money spent to influence public policy led to much bigger impacts than money spent individually on buying solar panels, recycling, shopping for organic produce, and so forth. I had long suspected this, but it was interesting to see it in print, and it makes perfect sense. Why? Because federal, state, and local governments control *trillions* of dollars while each of us controls, well, pocket change. That means that even small shifts in government policies can lead to vastly more dollars flowing toward environmental protection.

Do you know that the US Farm Bill is the single largest source of conservation funding in the United States? I didn't until I read an article about it in the American Bird Conservancy's *Bird Conservation* magazine. The 2022 Inflation Reduction Act alone poured *$20 billion* into Farm Bill conservation programs, including huge incentives for farmers and ranchers to restore and protect grassland ecosystems. This is not only vitally important to keep rural lands healthy and sustainable, it is crucial for grassland birds, which have witnessed staggering losses as their habitats have been gobbled up by industrial-scale agriculture and urban sprawl.

The Farm Bill amply illustrates the importance of steering our politicians in positive directions. Because it helps Americans from all walks of life, from farmers to urban-based birders, it also demonstrates the huge potential for engaging birder-citizens across the political spectrum to protect the environment.

I know, I know, politics is a hellhole, perhaps now more than ever. The tsunamis of disinformation, dark money, and extremism that wash through our political system have never been greater in my lifetime, and I don't expect them to abate anytime soon. Politics, though, is a necessary fact of life, and if you love birds and want them to stick around, you need to consider being involved.

I've already mentioned the importance of supporting groups that are working to save birds. Audubon, Cornell Lab, and American Bird Conservancy not only work directly to protect species and habitats, they produce reports and lobby representatives to shape budgets and laws in bird-friendly ways. These and other nonprofit and government agencies work together on many issues under the umbrella of the North American Bird Conservation Initiative (nacbi-us.org). It is because of efforts like

theirs that some people can now receive tax credits to install rooftop solar panels or buy used or new electric vehicles.

Beyond that, I encourage you to pay attention to what your own representatives, at both the local and national level, are doing. According to analysis by the Center for American Progress, our 2021 Congress included 109 representatives and 30 senators who were climate deniers and refused to accept overwhelming scientific evidence for human-caused climate change, and they made public statements to that effect. What's more, these representatives had collectively received $61 million from the coal, oil, and natural gas industries. I think I can safely say that these politicians are not protecting birds—or people, for that matter.

If you aren't sure where your representatives stand on climate change and other environmental issues, you can check out the scorecards from the League of Conservation Voters (lcv.org). A quick glance reveals that some representatives are way ahead of their colleagues when it comes to fighting for the environment. Before you vote, also get on candidates' websites and see what they have to say. Do they place environmental protection front and center, or do they just throw it in with a lot of other topics? Do they have an actual track record of working for the environment, whether they are currently in or out of office? Are they endorsed by any reputable conservation groups? These kinds of questions will help you pin down a candidate you can support.

## Activating Your Superpowers

Once you've educated yourself, as noted above, your efforts will depend on your time, resources, and conviction. Personally, I consider myself fairly middle-of-the-road when it comes to political activism. I identify candidates I want to support, and I put up candidate yard signs to annoy my neighbors. Then, in the big election cycles every two years, I pick out one candidate I am especially enthusiastic about and try to dedicate a few hours to volunteer for them. I stuff envelopes, assemble yard signs, and though I despise doing it, knock on doors and make telephone calls *on occasion*.

Each of us, though, has additional "superpowers" that we can bring to the bird-friendly political arena.

Maybe you are a member of the Rotary Club, Lion's Club, or another service organization? You could arrange a speaker to talk about birds or the environment in the current political cycle to help sway other members to support conservation-minded candidates.

My own superpower happens to be writing, and I usually write one or two letters to the editor each year promoting certain policies or candidates. In the last election cycle, though, I stepped up my game by submitting four actual op-ed pieces. These are longer and more detailed than letters to the editor, which often are limited to a couple of hundred words. With the longer op-eds, I was able to dive deeper into the bird-centric conservation issues I care about. I did not know if these would get published, but they did and, I hope, may have influenced other voters around the state.

In between election cycles, I write letters about all kinds of issues to Montana's congresspeople and senators. Many of them write back boasting about why they are going to do the exact *opposite* of what I ask, but I feel it's important for them to know that many of us out here disagree with their environmentally destructive policy decisions.

Individual voters from both parties care about conservation and often listen to reason, and birds appeal to people across the political spectrum. Some are duck hunters. Some are carrying binoculars and racking up life lists. Others enjoy seeing birds while out hunting deer or elk. Almost no one wants to see the environment poisoned or degraded or destroyed. If you can find a specific issue, such as wetlands protection or restoration of sage-grouse habitat, that appeals to voters in your area, collectively you may be able to sway even the most fossil-fuel-friendly officeholders to change their votes.

No matter who you vote for, remember that birders as a group have enormous power and ability to move the dial in favor of birds and, thus, our planet. I urge you to get involved and stay involved at whatever level you can. Every time you see a Dark-eyed Junco beneath your feeder or a flock of Snow Geese flying overhead, you will be glad that you did.

## CHAPTER 33

# The Fully Green Birder

The last few chapters have thrown a lot at you, but I wouldn't have done it if it weren't important. As the number of birders swells around the globe, so do the negative impacts of birders on the very animals and places we love. And yet I sometimes come across an attitude that because we are *watching birds* and appreciating nature, compared to, say, flying to Arizona to golf or go four-wheeling in the desert, that our impacts do not count. To that idea, I officially call "Bullshit!" If anything, birders should take our impacts on Earth more seriously and make greater efforts to reduce them.

In previous chapters, I mentioned different ways to explore the birds of the world while still striving to limit our carbon footprint:

- Piggybacking your birding excursions onto trips you were going to take anyway
- Opting to spend more time birding locally instead of in far-flung destinations
- Birding with others so that you can carpool or, better yet, bird by bicycle
- Choosing birding tours that minimize environmental impacts

These days, though, we stand poised at a new dawn in which reducing our impacts is even more possible thanks to the unfolding energy revolution. Advanced technology is rapidly allowing us to replace fossil fuels with wind, solar, geothermal, and other clean energy sources, as well as

# Plirding

Long before I became a birder, I got in the habit of picking up at least one or two pieces of trash whenever I went outdoors. This excellent habit had its roots in my days as a Boy Scout when I was taught, "Always leave a place better off than you found it."

Naturally, when I became a birder I continued this tradition and taught my son to do it as well. Imagine my surprise to learn that the habit has caught on with many birders—and that there's even a name for it: plirding, or "picking up litter while birding"!

With the number of hours birders spend out on the landscape, our potential to reduce the often hazardous trash littering our communities is enormous. Beyond that, plirding sets a wonderful example for others and makes us immediately feel that, yes, we can and do make the world a better place.

cleaner transport in the form of mass transit and electric cars and trucks. Unfortunately, as the world's second largest energy consumer, the United States has been woefully slow in making this transition, especially when it comes to transportation. While many nations, for instance, have already built fast, efficient, high-speed, cross-country rail networks, there is barely even talk of such a cohesive system here in the US. Similarly, most US cities don't even have rail-based subway or light-rail systems to serve their local populations. Thanks in large part to lobbying by the auto and fossil fuels industries, most of us remain dependent on cars to get around—and will be stuck with them for decades to come. That said, the advent of electric vehicles, or EVs, is good news, and as I mentioned in the last chapter, the federal government provides significant tax credits for both new and used EVs. I'd like to think that any birders with sufficient finances will be first in line to buy these game-changing vehicles.

# Coffee and Chocolate for Birds

One of the most fun ways to "go green" is to plug in to consumer habits. Being a rabid chocoholic, I should know! It's an inconvenient fact that both cacao and coffee plantations often replace natural forests with vast biological deserts strictly devoted to producing these sought-after comestibles. Scientists and conservationists at the Smithsonian Migratory Bird Center (nationalzoo.si.edu/migratory-birds) have targeted both industries to make them more bird- and ecofriendly by encouraging "shade-grown" agricultural methods.

"Sun-grown" cacao and coffee plantations are those in which all natural vegetation—including tropical rainforest—is removed and replaced by single-species crop plants. At least in the short run, these plantations produce higher yields, but in the process they destroy the ecosystem for other plants and animals. In contrast, shade-grown farms retain or plant a wide mix of other plants, creating a canopy and understory that at least partly mimics natural systems.

Numerous studies have demonstrated that shade-grown farms support dramatically higher biodiversity than their sun-grown analogs, while earning greater profits for farmers. They also offer many additional benefits such as reducing soil erosion and curtailing the need for fertilizers and pesticides.

Not surprisingly, these kinds of farms benefit birds directly. While shade-grown coffee initiatives have outpaced sustainable cacao initiatives, the latter are also  expanding. To learn more, look up "shade-grown coffee" on the Smithsonian Migratory Bird Center's website. Meanwhile, keep an eye out for the official "Bird Friendly" certification the next time you need to stock up on your favorite guilty pleasures. In the process, you'll make them a lot more digestible!

Rooftop solar panels are another great development in the battle against climate change, and, again, the federal government offers generous tax credits for these systems as well. This sets up an ideal situation in which birders can start charging their electric vehicles using their own rooftop solar panels, and I know several who do this already.

Naturally, buying electric cars and solar panels costs money and is beyond the means of many of us, but almost all of us have additional opportunities to reduce our carbon footprints and impacts on birds and the planet:

- Eat less meat to free up immense swaths of agricultural land for carbon-gobbling forests and grasslands.
- Vote for efficient electric rail systems in urban and suburban areas—and use them.
- Buy more locally grown food, reducing the amount of fuel needed to transport it.
- Get an energy audit of your home to identify places that need better sealing or insulation.
- Replace stoves, heaters, and other appliances that use natural gas with electric models.
- Install a heat pump for heating and cooling your house.

Tax incentives, by the way, are available to help with the last three items. Of course, not every one of us can or will do every one of these things, but the more we do, the better off we all will be, including the birds among us. Fellow birders, we get only one shot at this, and as a community, we can both improve the situation for everyone and inspire others to do the same.

Let's get on it.

# WRAP-UP: FINAL WINGBEATS

By happy coincidence I find myself finishing the first draft of this book on December 29—only two days before New Year's Eve. For birders, this is a time to reflect on the wonderful birds we've seen in the past twelve months, relive our many adventures, and think about those really special sightings—new species for our life lists, perhaps, or birds that we never expected or thought we would see.

This year, thanks to an unexpected family vacation to New York, a work trip to Florida, and a road trip driving Braden to his summer job in California, I observed thirty-five new lifers. These included some really spectacular species I wondered if I'd ever get to see: Elegant Trogon, Varied Bunting, Sulphur-bellied Flycatcher, Scott's Oriole, and Red-faced, Magnolia, Prairie, Cape May, and Black-throated Blue Warblers.

Beyond my new sightings, the year offered an array of adventures unlike any in my previous experience. I climbed a 7,500-foot Montana ridge to watch migrating raptors zoom past. I sat up late with biologists trying to catch and band Common Poorwills and Flammulated Owls. I helped band and record migrating thrushes, warblers, and other songbirds as they prepared to head south for the winter. I visited Florida's Eglin Air Force Base, where scientists have done an amazing job restoring longleaf pine ecosystems to help Red-cockaded Woodpeckers and many other species.

As wonderful as these adventures were, however, it was the experiences with my son that I cherish the most. Birding around Montana, catching spring migration in New York's Central Park, returning to Arizona for the first time in six years—these are all adventures Braden and I will never forget, and without birding, they never would have happened.

I share this with you not to boast or make anyone jealous, but to drive home the point of what's possible when you become a birder. Ten years ago, I could never have imagined all of the ways that strapping on binoculars and tramping through woods and prairies would enrich my life both personally and professionally.

Believe me, it can do the same for you. Whether you explore your neighborhood or find ways to visit far-flung destinations, I guarantee that carving out time to watch birds will make your life better. It will make you healthier and happier. It will keep your brain sharper. It will help you forge new relationships—and, with luck, deepen the connections you already have. It can even give you a new sense of purpose, making the planet better for yourself, the birds, and everyone around you.

Wherever you are with your birding interests, I hope that this book has provided you with at least a bit of guidance, encouragement, ideas, inspiration, and entertainment. As a new year approaches, though, it is not *just* a time for reflection. It is also a time to start thinking about next year's birding goals and adventures. So for now, fellow Boomers and everyone else reading this, I will bid you a fond farewell so that both of us can start imagining where birds might take us.

I hope to see you out there.

The End

# THANK YOU, BIRDERS AND ALL!

Thanking everyone who helped me with this project is perhaps the most intimidating aspect of the entire book. I owe gratitude to so many people that writing this section may push me over my word count, disqualifying me from ever publishing another book, and sinking me into a pit of professional despair. But since I mentioned publishing, let's start with Kate Rogers, the wonderful editor in chief of Mountaineers Books who immediately found merit in this idea and fully supported it from the get-go—even if she did say I was being too funny in places! Huge thanks also to the rest of Mountaineers Books' terrific staff, who did an amazing job with my last book and I'm sure will outdo themselves with this one. You all are awesome! My special gratitude goes to Beth Jusino, who patiently edited *Boomers* and made countless terrific suggestions for improving it. Thank you, Beth! Further accolades to freelance editor Laura Whittemore (Kingbird Editorial), who did an amazing job copyediting the book and helped take it to the next level.

On the birding front, I must first thank my son, Braden Collard, who shared the vast majority of adventures that led to this book, put up with me patiently throughout, and who kindly read over and corrected parts of the manuscript. A shout-out to our friend Nick Ramsey, another gifted young birder who taught me much of what I know. I also *must* thank the birders of the Montana Birding and Redpolling Facebook groups for patiently—often enthusiastically—responding to my research polls and questions. You guys and gals are a lot of fun!

Speaking of teaching, I have been especially fortunate to have met and spoken with many ornithologists who have taken time—in some cases a *lot* of time—to share their expertise and explain it in ways that even a Boomer like me can understand. These include Dick Hutto, Erick Greene, Bruce Byers, Debbie Leick, Megan Fylling, Dan Casey, Kate Stone, Tricia Rodriguez, William Blake, and Holly Garrod.

Regarding gear, instruments, equity, medical advice, and a range of other topics, I am indebted to Uschi Carpenter, Glenn Olsen, Helen Drummond, Steve Flood, Roger Kohn, Eric Dawson, Harold Mills, Kristi DuBois, Harold Underdown, Malcolm Hodges, Jack Grove, Paul Queneau, Lang Elliott, Zak Pohlen, Tony Higuera, Stephen Spann, Alex Sundvall, Harley Winfrey, and Christian Roberts.

Finally, I'd like to thank my wife, Amy, and my youngest, Tessa, for never wavering in their support of me, my birding, my writing, and my passion for nature and travel. I love you!

And if there's anyone I forgot? Well, I am truly, abjectly sorry. Then again, I'm a Boomer. You can't hold my aging brain fully accountable. Just remind me that I forgot to mention you, and I'll buy you a White Russian the next time we watch *The Big Lebowski* together. The birds abide!

# RESOURCES

Once birding hooks you, it has this wonderful way of seeping into all aspects of your life including your literary habits, intellectual pursuits, and entertainment. Not surprisingly, once you start becoming "bird aware," you'll find gobs of resources perched at your fingertips.

Below is a compilation of most of the resources I mentioned in this book, plus a few others that you might appreciate. While I have direct experience with most of them, some have been recommended to me by other people or in various publications I have read. Although I hope they steer you in the right directions, I make no warranties and urge you to do your own due diligence.

**I SHOULD NOTE** that I did not receive any fees, products, or services from any of the companies or individuals mentioned in this book—damn it! I will try harder next time.

## Bird Conservation Groups

Here are groups I think are doing the most to help protect birds and our planet. Two that I did not call out enough are the US Fish and Wildlife Service and the National Oceanic and Atmospheric Administration, which oversee the protection of endangered and threatened species, including birds. And yes, we do need big government agencies! You will undoubtedly discover other local, regional, national, and international groups having a positive impact on birds as you continue your birding career.

**American Bird Conservancy**
   https://abcbirds.org
**American Birding Association**
   www.aba.org

**BirdLife International**
  https://birdlife.org
**Center for Biological Diversity**
  www.biologicaldiversity.org
**Conservation International**
  www.conservation.org
**Cornell Lab of Ornithology**
  www.birds.cornell.edu/home
**Ducks Unlimited**
  www.ducks.org
**National Audubon Society**
  Regional, state, and local Audubon chapters
  www.audubon.org
**National Oceanic and Atmospheric Administration**
  www.fisheries.noaa.gov/national/science-data/seabirds
**The Peregrine Fund**
  www.peregrinefund.org
**Union of Concerned Scientists**
  www.ucsusa.org
**US Fish and Wildlife Service**
  https://fws.gov

## Books

Being an author, I naturally have to share my favorite birding resources, books. And I'm not talking about poorly conceived, self-published ebooks available exclusively on tablets and the other devices implanted in our nervous systems. I'm talking about *real* books that you can use and abuse, thumb through and write in, browse and ponder. Thankfully, these primitive devices still exist, and under the category of birds and birding, in great abundance. The bad news? I would need to write an entire book to give you a complete tour of the great bird-related books available. Before I begin, in fact, I'd like to apologize ahead of time to the many great books and authors I do not have space to include here.

Ackerman, Jennifer. *The Bird Way: A New Look at How Birds Talk, Work, Play, Parent, and Think*. New York: Penguin Press, 2020.

———. *The Genius of Birds*. New York: Penguin Press, 2016.

Bannick, Paul. *Great Gray Owl: A Visual History*. Seattle: Mountaineers Books, 2020.

———. *Owl: A Year in the Lives of North American Owls*. Seattle: Braided River, 2016.

———. *The Owl and the Woodpecker: Encounters with North America's Most Iconic Birds*. With a foreword by Tony Angell. Seattle: Mountaineers Books, 2008.

———. *Snowy Owl: A Visual History*. Seattle: Mountaineers Books, 2020.

Barber, Lynn E. *Big Years, Biggest States: Birding in Texas and Alaska*. College Station: Texas A&M University Press, 2020.

Brooke, Michael. *Far From Land: The Mysterious Lives of Seabirds*. Princeton, NJ: Princeton University Press, 2018.

Collard, Sneed B., III. *Warblers & Woodpeckers: A Father-Son Big Year of Birding*. Seattle: Mountaineers Books, 2018.

Cooper, Christian. *Better Living Through Birding: Notes from a Black Man in the Natural World*. New York: Penguin Random House, 2023.

Gallagher, Tim. *Imperial Dreams: Tracking the Imperial Woodpecker Through the Wild Sierra Madre*. New York: Atria Books, 2013.

Hammer, Joshua. *The Falcon Thief: A True Tale of Adventure, Treachery, and the Hunt for the Perfect Bird*. New York: Simon & Schuster, 2020.

Hashimoto, Molly. *Birds of the West: An Artist's Guide*. Seattle: Skipstone, 2019.

Kaizar, Sarah, with A. Scott Meiser. *Rare Air: Endangered Birds, Bats, Butterflies & Bees*. Seattle: Skipstone, 2023.

Kaufman, Kenn. *Kingbird Highway: The Biggest Year in the Life of an Extreme Birder*. Boston: Houghton Mifflin, 1997.

Kroodsma, Donald. *Birdsong for the Curious Naturalist: Your Guide to Listening*. Boston: Mariner Books, 2020.

Lanham, J. Drew. *The Home Place: Memoirs of a Colored Man's Love Affair with Nature*. Minneapolis: Milkweed Editions, 2017.

Long, Kim. *What Birds Eat: How to Preserve the Natural Diet of Behavior of North American Birds*. Seattle: Skipstone, 2020.

Low, Tim. *Where Song Began: Australia's Birds and How They Changed the World*. New Haven, CT: Yale University Press, 2016.

Meiburg, Jonathan. *A Most Remarkable Creature: The Hidden Life and Epic Journey of the World's Smartest Birds of Prey*. New York: Alfred A. Knopf, 2021.

Nicolson, Adam. *The Seabird's Cry: The Lives and Loves of the Planet's Great Ocean Voyagers*. New York: Henry Holt, 2018.

Obmascik, Mark. *The Big Year: A Tale of Man, Nature, and Fowl Obsession*. New York: Free Press, 2004.

Peterson, Roger Tory. *Wild America: The Record of a 30,000-mile Journey Around the Continent by a Distinguished Naturalist and His British Colleague*. Boston: Houghton Mifflin, 1955.

Ruth, Maria Mudd. *Rare Bird: Pursuing the Mystery of the Marbled Murrelet*. Seattle: Mountaineers Books, 2005.

Sibley, David Allen. *The Sibley Guide to Birds*. 2nd ed. New York: Alfred A. Knopf, 2014.

Skaife, Christopher. *The Ravenmaster: My Life with the Ravens at the Tower of London*. New York: Farrar, Straus, and Giroux, 2018.

Tallamy, Douglas W. *Nature's Best Hope: A New Approach to Conservation That Starts in Your Yard*. Portland, OR: Timber Press, 2019.

Vyn, Gerrit, and The Cornell Lab. *Photography Birds: Field Techniques and the Art of the Image*. Seattle: Mountaineers Books, 2020.

West, George C. *A Birder's Guide to Alaska*. Colorado Springs: American Birding Association, 2008.

## Bird-Related Magazines

Until recently I, like many people, believed that magazines had gone extinct sometime in the first decade of this century. Turns out, bird and birding magazines are alive and well! Furthermore, they are a great way to keep up with the latest bird discoveries, great birding gear, bird identification tips, bird conservation, and events and locations that cater to avid and casual birders alike. I urge you to subscribe to a few, some of which come with annual memberships to birding organizations and some of which stand alone. By doing so, you will (a) make yourself a much better birder and (b) help support a vital avenue of communication within the birding community.

- *Audubon* (available for additional fee with membership to National Audubon)
- *Bird Watcher's Digest (BWD)*
- *Birding* (with membership to the American Birding Association)
- *BirdLife* (with membership to BirdLife International—Braden's favorite magazine)
- *Birds & Blooms* (a magazine for gardeners with the aim of attracting birds and insects)

FOR THOSE WITH an academic bent, you can also subscribe to dozens of scientific journals catering to almost every aspect of bird study and every geographic area of the world. These include huge journals such as *Ornithology*, published by the American Ornithological Society, and smaller, more regional journals such as *Western Birds* published by Western Field Ornithologists. I have used a number of these when researching my children's books about birds, and many should be available through your local university library if you are fortunate to have one nearby.

## Bird-Related Websites

"Birdzillions" of bird-related websites now fill the electronic universe, and you will no doubt discover plenty of your own. You might even start one yourself like Braden and I did! The list below includes most of the sites I mentioned earlier—especially ones I refer to a lot—as well as a few others you might find useful.

**All About Birds, Cornell Lab of Ornithology**
www.allaboutbirds.org

**Audubon Bird Migration Explorer**
https://explorer.audubon.org
**Audubon Guide to North American Birds**
www.audubon.org/bird-guide
**Audubon Plants for Birds**
www.audubon.org/plantsforbirds
**Birdability**
www.birdability.org
**Birdability Location Explorer**
https://gis.audubon.org/birdability
**Bird of the Day challenge**
www.morgantingley.com/botd
**Birds of the World, Cornell Lab of Ornithology**
https://birdsoftheworld.org/bow/home
**Bird Song Hero game**
https://academy.allaboutbirds.org/bird-song-hero
**Bird Watching HQ**
https://birdwatchinghq.com
**Black Birders Week**
www.blackafinstem.com
**Black Swamp Bird Observatory**
www.bsbo.org
**Buteo Books**
www.buteobooks.com
**Digital Photography Review (DPReview)**
www.dpreview.com
**eBird, Cornell Lab of Ornithology**
https://ebird.org/home
**Fatbirder**
https://fatbirder.com
**Fathersonbirding.com (my blog site)**
https://fathersonbirding.com

**Garden for Wildlife (National Wildlife Federation)**
  https://gardenforwildlife.com
**Great Backyard Bird Count**
  www.birdcount.org
**Great Texas Wildlife Trails**
  https://tpwd.texas.gov/huntwild/wildlife/wildlife-trails
**Hear Birds Again**
  https://hearbirdsagain.org
**Houston Audubon**
  https://houstonaudubon.org
**The International Union for the Conservation of Nature Red List**
  www.iucnredlist.org
**League of Conservation Voters**
  www.lcv.org
**National Council on Aging**
  www.ncoa.org
**Princeton University Press**
  https://press.princeton.edu
**Project FeederWatch**
  www.feederwatch.org
**Smithsonian Migratory Bird Center (shade-grown coffee and cacao)**
  https://nationalzoo.si.edu/migratory-birds

## Bird-Related Podcasts

There are so many bird-related podcasts out there that I'm not even going to attempt to round them up. I have two reasons for this. One is that if I did, the list would be out of date by the time you are reading this, and probably require so many pages that many of Earth's forests would have to be cut down simply to list them all. The second is that I generally refuse to listen to podcasts. I know, I know. This makes me a Neanderthal of a human being and I do not attempt to justify it. I simply choose to spend my time elsewhere.

That said, many people swear that podcasts are excellent sources of bird information and that they find them very enjoyable. Here are a few that others have recommended. For more suggestions, simply do a web search for "best bird podcasts."

**American Birding Podcast**
  www.aba.org/podcast
**BirdNote (blog and podcast)**
  www.birdnote.org
**Voices of a Flyway: Exploring the Mississippi Flyway's Place-Based Stories and Sounds**
  https://voicesofaflyway.com/explore
**The Weekly Bird Report with Mark Faherty**
  www.capeandislands.org/podcast/weekly-bird-report

## Bird-Related Apps
You may run out of memory on your phone before you run out of apps to download. All are worth exploring, but in case you need to "economize" on space, the three I use most often are eBird, Merlin, and Sibley.

**The Audubon Bird Guide App**
**Audubon Owls Guide**
**BirdNET**
**Chirp! Bird Songs & Calls USA**
**eBird (works in tandem with web version of eBird)**
**Hear Birds Again**
**iBird Pro**
**iNaturalist**
**Larkwire**
**Merlin (contains Sound ID)**
**Raptor ID**
**The Sibley Guide to Birds 2.0**

The Warbler Guide
World of Wings (fun birding game)

## Sources

In the main chapters, I mentioned several articles, podcasts, blogs, and reports, and you can look up any you choose, but here are links to what I consider the most important ones to follow up on:

"Affinity and Identity in the QBNA with Jennifer Rycenga & Michael Retter." www.aba.org/affinity-and-identity-in-the-queer-birders -of-north-america-with-jennifer-rycenga-michael-retter/.

American Bird Conservancy. "Preventing Bird Collisions at Home." https://abcbirds.org/glass-collisions/stop-birds-hitting-windows.

"Birding While Black with J. Drew Lanham." www.aba.org/birding -while-black-with-j-drew-lanham/.

Furtman, Michael. "All About Owl Baiting." www.michaelfurtman.com /On_Owl_Baiting.htm.

Groo, Melissa. "Getting Closer." *Outdoor Photographer*, March 7, 2022. www.outdoorphotographer.com/pro-perspectives/melissa -groo/getting-closer/.

Kays, R., et al. "The Small Home Ranges and Large Local Ecological Impacts of Pet Cats" *Animal Conservation* 23, no. 5 (March 11, 2020). https://zslpublications.onlinelibrary.wiley.com/doi/abs/10.1111 /acv.12563 or https://gwern.net/doc/cat/psychology/2020-kays.pdf.

Lanham, J. Drew. "9 Rules for the Black Birdwatcher." *Orion*, October 25, 2013. https://orionmagazine.org/article/9-rules-for-the-black -birdwatcher/.

Loss, S., T. Will, and P. Mara. "The Impact of Free-Ranging Domestic Cats on Wildlife of the United States." *Nature Communications* 4, no. 1396 (2013). www.nature.com/articles/ncomms2380.

NABCI. State of the Birds report. www.stateofthebirds.org.

## Birding Equipment, Books, and Supply Vendors

I have had positive transactions with most of the vendors below, while the others have been recommended to me, but as with any commercial transactions, your experiences may differ and I make no warranties.

**Adorama (used camera equipment)**
www.adorama.com
**B&H Photo (photo, camera equipment)**
www.bhphotovideo.com
**Buteo Books (bird-related bookstore)**
www.buteobooks.com
**KEH (used camera equipment)**
www.keh.com
**Land Sea & Sky (scopes, binoculars, etc.)**
https://landseaskyco.com
**Lensrentals (camera and video equipment rental)**
www.lensrentals.com
**Sparrowtraps.net (bird traps)**
https://sparrowtraps.net
**Wild Birds Unlimited (range of feeders, nest boxes, and general bird and birding supplies)**
www.wbu.com

# ABOUT THE AUTHOR

Sneed B. Collard III graduated with honors in marine biology from University of California–Berkeley and earned a masters in scientific instrumentation from UC Santa Barbara. He is the author of more than ninety acclaimed children's books including *Border Crossings*, winner of the prestigious 2024 Orbis Pictus Award for children's nonfiction literature. His two other adult books include the humorous, award-winning memoir *Warblers & Woodpeckers: A Father-Son Big Year of Birding*, also published by Mountaineers Books, and the travel guide *First-Time Japan: A Step-by-Step Guide for the Independent Traveler*.

In addition to writing books, Sneed is a regular contributor of nature and travel features to *Bird Watcher's Digest*, *Big Sky Journal*, and *Montana Outdoors* magazines, and he and his son Braden share their birding adventures on the blog, fathersonbirding.com. When he is not birding and writing, Sneed is a popular speaker and trip leader at schools, conferences, and birding festivals. To learn more about him, his books, and presentations, check out www.sneedbcollardiii.com.

MOUNTAINEERS BOOKS

SKIPSTONE   BRAIDED RIVER

recreation · lifestyle · conservation

**MOUNTAINEERS BOOKS,** including its two imprints, Skipstone and Braided River, is a leading publisher of quality outdoor recreation, sustainability, and conservation titles. As a 501(c)(3) nonprofit, we are committed to supporting the environmental and educational goals of our organization by providing expert information on human-powered adventure, sustainable practices at home and on the trail, and preservation of wilderness.

Our publications are made possible through the generosity of donors, and through sales of 700 titles on outdoor recreation, sustainable lifestyle, and conservation. To donate, purchase books, or learn more, visit us online:

### MOUNTAINEERS BOOKS

1001 SW Klickitat Way, Suite 201 • Seattle, WA 98134
800-553-4453 • mbooks@mountaineersbooks.org • www.mountaineersbooks.org

*An independent nonprofit publisher since 1960*

### YOU MAY ALSO LIKE:

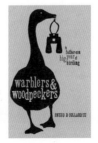